THE BOOK OF KUDZU

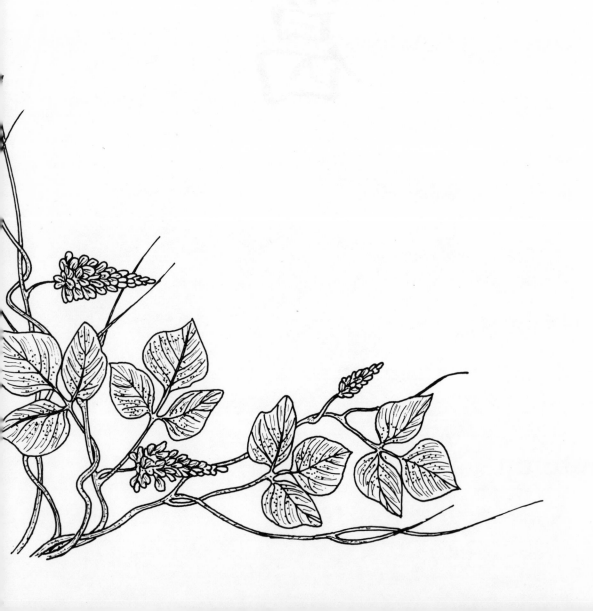

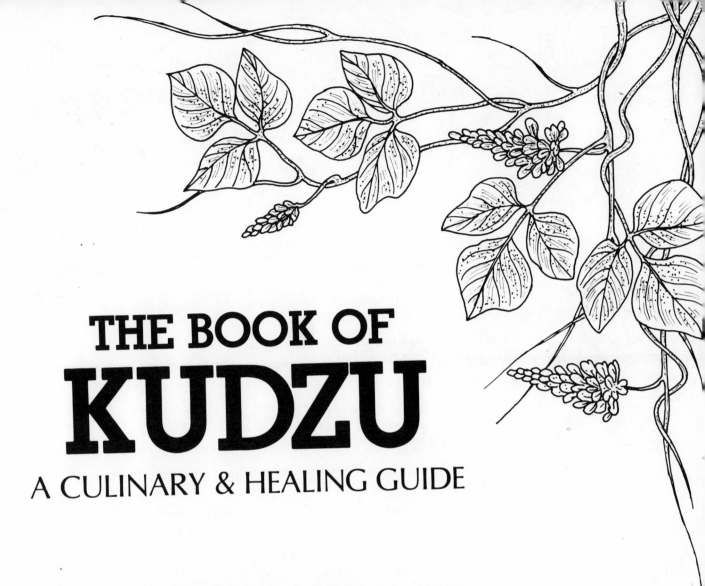

THE BOOK OF
KUDZU
A CULINARY & HEALING GUIDE

WILLIAM SHURTLEFF & AKIKO AOYAGI
Illustrated by Akiko Aoyagi

Autumn Press

By the Same Authors:
The Book of Tofu
The Book of Miso

PUBLISHED BY AUTUMN PRESS, INC.
WITH EDITORIAL OFFICES AT
7 LITTELL ROAD,
BROOKLINE, MASSACHUSETTS 02146

DISTRIBUTED IN THE UNITED STATES
BY RANDOM HOUSE, INC. AND IN
CANADA BY RANDOM HOUSE OF CANADA, LTD.

LIBRARY OF CONGRESS CATALOG CARD NUMBER: 77-074891
ISBN:0-394-73427-0

TYPESET AT DNH, CAMBRIDGE, MASSACHUSETTS.
PRINTED IN THE UNITED STATES OF AMERICA.

COVER ILLUSTRATION BY AKIKO AOYAGI.

BOOK DESIGN AND TYPOGRAPHY BY BEVERLY STISKIN.

Contents

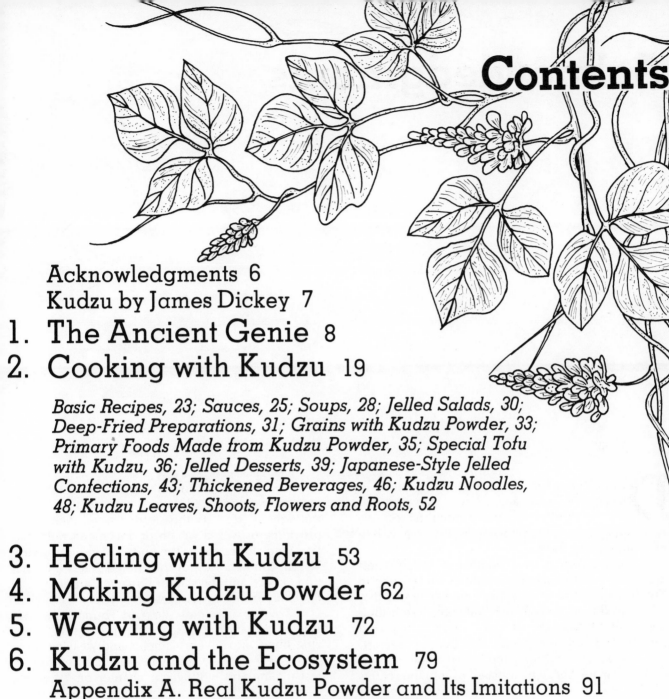

Acknowledgments

DURING OUR four years of studying kudzu in Japan and Taiwan and our two years of studying it throughout the United States, we received help from numerous specialists. We wish to give our sincere thanks . . .

To the owners of a number of Japan's best restaurants and confectionery shops specializing in the preparation of fine cuisine from kudzu powder, who allowed us to visit their kitchens, watch their chefs and craftspeople at work, study their prized recipes, and sample the delectable fruits of their art.

To Ms. Lima Ohsawa and Messrs. Hideo Omori and Hidemasa Abé, who initiated us into the secrets of the use of kudzu powder and kudzu root in traditional, natural healing and explained the history of their use as a medicine. And to Noboru Muramoto, Michio and Aveline Kushi, and Herman and Cornellia Aihara, who have brought these medicinal teachings to the West.

To the directors of each of Japan's major producers of kudzu powder, who kindly and patiently answered our many questions, guided us through their shops, and provided detailed explanations of their traditional and modern production methods. Special gratitude is due to Mr. Makoto Taguchi of Hiro Hachido Shoten. And to Messrs. Akiyoshi Kazama and Alkan Yamaguchi for helping us track down information about the production of kudzu powder in Japan.

To the hundreds of agricultural research experts, farmers, and lovers or haters of kudzu throughout the southeastern United States for providing us with a wealth of documents, information, and stories about the kudzu plant in America. To Mr. John Hudson of the United States Information Service and the staff of *Organic Gardening and Farming* for their special research help.

To Ann Foster of the Yurt Foundation, who studied the ancient arts of hand-processing kudzu vine fibers into silken filaments and weaving these into lovely textiles, and who played a key role in researching and writing our chapter on "Weaving with Kudzu." To Moichi Kawadé, Japan's foremost authority of kudzu cloth (and Ann's teacher), who showed us his two excellent color films on the subject and went out of his way to help us in obtaining illustrative and historical material. To Marjie Short for her prize-winning, Academy Award-nominated color film on kudzu, James Dickey for his famous poem on kudzu, and Jimmy Carter for his personal wish to "let it grow."

Finally, a special measure of appreciation is due to Mr. Tyler Smith and Ms. Sandy MacDonald, whose careful editorial guidance and sound judgment played a key role in the creation of this work.

KUDZU

—James Dickey

Japan invades. Far Eastern vines.
Run from the clay banks they are

Supposed to keep from eroding,
Up telephone poles,
Which rear, half out of leafage,
As though they would shriek,
Like things smothered by their own
Green, mindless, unkillable ghosts.
In Georgia, the legend says
That you must close your windows

At night to keep it out of the house.
The glass is tinged with green, even so,

As the tendrils crawl over the fields.
The night the kudzu has
Your pasture, you sleep like the dead.
Silence has grown Oriental,
And you cannot step upon ground:
Your leg plunges somewhere
It should not, it never should be,
Disappears, and waits to be struck

Anywhere between sole and kneecap:
For when the kudzu comes,

The snakes do, and weave themselves
Among its lengthening vines,
Their spade heads resting on leaves,
Growing also, in earthly power
And the huge circumstance of concealment.
One by one the cows stumble in,
Drooling a hot green froth,
And die, seeing the wood of their stalls

Strain to break into leaf.
In your closed house, with the vine

Tapping your window like lightning,
You remember what tactics to use.
In the wrong yellow fog-light of dawn
You herd them in, the hogs,
Head down in their hairy fat,
The meaty troops, to the pasture.
The leaves of the kudzu quake
With the serpents fear, inside

The meadow ringed with men
Holding stocks, on the country roads.

The hogs disappear in the leaves.
The sound is intense, subhuman,
Nearly human with purposive rage.
There is no terror
Sound from the snakes.
No one can see the desperate, futile
Striking under the leaf heads.
Now and then, the flash of a long

Living vine, a cold belly
Leaps up, torn apart, then falls

Under the tussling surface.
You have won, and wait for frost,
When, at the merest touch
Of cold, the kudzu turns
Black, withers inward and dies,
Leaving a mass of brown strings
Like the wires of a gigantic switchboard.
You open your windows,

With the lightning restored to the sky
And no leaves rising to bury

You alive inside your frail house,
And you think, in the opened cold,
Of the surface of things and its terrors,
And of the mistaken, mortal
Arrogance of the snakes
As the vines, growing insanely, sent
Great powers into their bodies
And the freedom to strike without warning:

From them, though they killed
Your cattle, such energy also flowed

To you from the knee-high meadow
(It was as though you had
A green sword twined among
The veins of your growing right arm—
Such strength as you would not believe
If you stood alone in a proper
Shaved field among your safe cows—):
Came in through your closed

Leafy windows and almighty sleep
And prospered, till rooted out.

1. The Ancient Genie

KUDZU IS an ancient genie that delights in the endless, shape-shifting play of transformation—it is at times a prankster, at times a selfless servant. Its forms and uses are rich and varied, differing from country to country throughout the world.

What are Kudzu and Kudzu Powder?

Kudzu (pronounced *KUD*-zoo in the Deep South and *KOOD*-zoo most everywhere else) is a prolific leguminous vine of the genus *Pueraria*, native to the Orient; the Japanese call it *kuzu* (*KOO-zoo*).* Introduced to the United States in 1876, kudzu now grows more prolifically throughout the Deep South than in any other part of the world.

"Kudzu powder" (a literal translation of the Japanese term *kuzu-ko*) is a remarkable starchlike extract of the kudzu root; now sold in natural food stores throughout America, it is sometimes labeled simply "kuzu." The powder comes in crumbly white chunks and has been used in Japan since ancient times as a key ingredient in fine cuisine and as an unusually effective natural medicine. The root itself, which may grow to a length of 7 feet or more and weigh as much as 440 pounds, is also diced and dried for use as the primary ingredient in several of East Asia's most esteemed medicinal teas.

In the South, kudzu's devotees point out that the plant combines the virtues of several species: it has long been used for erosion control, livestock

* For the sake of uniformity, when referring to Japanese terms (such as recipe titles), we will consistently use the American spelling "kudzu."

fodder, as a honey source, and as an ornamental vine, whose lovely wisteria-like flowers emit a sweet fragrance like that of crushed grapes. Moreover, its leguminous roots host nitrogen-fixing bacteria which enrich the soil by providing a free and continuous supply of natural fertilizer. Originally wild, kudzu is unquestionably a superplant, for it thrives without fertilizers, pesticides, irrigation, cultivation, replanting, or even care. The key question remains, however: "Is kudzu super-good or super-bad?"

During the warm months, almost anywhere you travel south of the Mason-Dixon line or east of Texas, and especially in the Deep South, you can see great billowing waves of kudzu washing over highway embankments and invading farmlands in a riot of luxuriant foliage. In its relentless search for more room, kudzu has spread like wildfire across the landscape and generally proved itself to be an unstoppable nuisance. It climbs and suffocates trees, transforming them into huge emerald hulks, then goes on to engulf road signs, telephone poles, and abandoned dwellings in a sea of leafy green tendrils. During the cold months, its appearance suddenly changes. In the words of the poet James Dickey (*Poems 1957–1967*):

> . . . at the merest touch
> Of cold, the kudzu turns
> Black, withers inward and dies,
> Leaving a mass of brown strings
> Like the wires of a gigantic switchboard.

Whereas the Japanese practice a kind of agricultural judo on kudzu, turning its overflowing energy to their advantage, American farmers today, unaware of the "white gold" buried in the roots, usually curse and try to eradicate this hardy perennial. They do not realize that the "green menace" is, in fact, one of Japan's most honored wild plants, just asking to have its roots harvested and processed into what could become America's finest-quality cooking starch and natural herbal medicine.

As versatile as it is delicious, kudzu powder can be used like arrowroot or cornstarch as a colloidal thickener in sauces or soups, or as a crispy coating for deep-fried foods; like agar or gelatin, it can also serve as a jelling agent, imparting delicate texture and prized flavor to numerous treats and desserts. In Japan about 85 percent of the more than 750,000 pounds of kudzu powder produced each year is used in the preparation of traditional confections. It is also used in the commercial preparation of satin-smooth Kudzu Noodles. And some Japanese naturo-paths have gone so far as to recommend kudzu powder as a substitute for brown rice or other grains as the primary food in a healing diet.

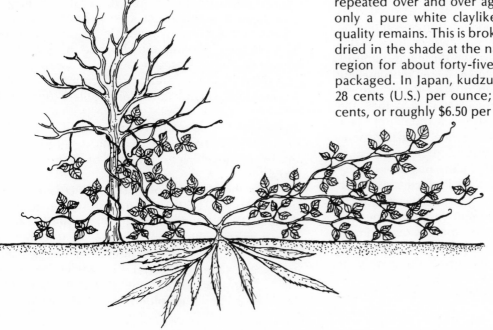

Pre-packaged kudzu powder

Now widely available in the West at reasonable prices, kudzu powder is imported from Japan in large quantities (about forty thousand 4-ounce pack-ages yearly) and sold at many natural food stores and Japanese markets. It will, we hope, soon be pro-duced in America, since kudzu can be cultivated in virtually any climate and kudzu powder can easily be made on a home, community, or commercial scale, using the roots of locally grown plants.

Although the terms "kudzu powder" or "kuzu" are often translated in English dictionaries as "arrowroot," the two foods should not be con-fused. Arrowroot, which comes from the tropical West Indies, produces a starch that, upon micro-scopic analysis, is distinctly different. Although less expensive, it lacks kudzu powder's medicinal value and is inferior in both texture and flavor as a jelling agent and coating for deep-fried foods.

In Japan, the roots of the wild kudzu vine are quite difficult and expensive to gather. From early December until late March, during the coldest part of the year, when the plant has finished its annual growth, and the starch and life force are drawn down into the roots, men go into the mountains, some-times walking as much as 2 or 3 miles cross-country until they find mature plants. Frequently working in dense underbrush, they dig out the long and tangled roots with a mountain hoe, cut them into 3-foot lengths with a handsaw, and backpack them in huge bundles down to a waiting truck which transports them to a shop for processing. The tough, fibrous roots are first crushed to a pulp, then mixed with cold mountain water to form a slurry, which is filtered through fine-mesh screens to remove the crude fiber. The milky water is allowed to stand in large tanks, where the kudzu starch settles to form layers; the lighter impurities rise to the surface while the remaining fibers and denser materials sink to the bottom. The upper and lower impure layers are removed, and the precious central layer is again washed and allowed to settle. This process is repeated over and over again for sixteen days until only a pure white claylike essence of the highest quality remains. This is broken into small squares and dried in the shade at the natural temperature of the region for about forty-five more days before being packaged. In Japan, kudzu powder retails for about 28 cents (U.S.) per ounce; in America it sells for 41 cents, or roughly $6.50 per pound.

The kudzu plant

JAPAN

Hokkaido

Kyoto

Tokyo

Kakegawa

Ouda

Kyushu

Nara

Kagoshima

Yoshino

Kudzu in Japan

Kudzu is one of Japan's most pervasive wild plants, and kudzu powder is thought to have been the country's first cooking starch and jelling agent (it is still its finest). Mention of the plant first appears in the *Manyoshu*, a colorful collection of poems compiled in about 600 A.D.; the *Wamyosho*, written during the ninth century, describes the leaves being used as a wild vegetable. Farmers in the mountains of central and southern Japan purportedly began extracting the starch and preparing the chunky powder from kudzu roots for use in home cookery and as a natural medicine as early as 1200 A.D., working on a small scale and with simple equipment. Documents show that fine cloth woven from kudzu fibers was in production by the thirteenth century, and by about 1610 the first commercial shop making kudzu powder was opened in Nara Prefecture. At the beginning of the Tokugawa era (circa 1620) the *Ryori Monogatari* [The story of cooking] gave recipes for Kudzu Mochi and Grilled Kudzu Mochi, in which kudzu powder was used to make cakes resembling those of pounded glutinous rice.

Since ancient times, Nara Prefecture, located south of Kyoto, has been famous for its kudzu powder. The area around Mount Yoshino, famed for its thousand cherry trees, is so closely associated with the product that many Japanese today refer to all kudzu powder as "Yoshino kudzu." The powder is said to have been first sold as a souvenir to cherry blossom viewers, mountain climbers, and pilgrims.

And, in fact, the plant is said to have taken its name from a village in Yoshino County.

In Japan, the ancient genie has a multitude of unique forms and virtues that are known to people in all walks of life.

For the gourmet, kudzu powder appears in the world of *Shojin Ryori* (Zen Temple Cookery), where it prefers a guise of elegant refinement, a sense of the aristocratic and the traditional. At Japan's finest temple restaurants, it is likely to appear at the beginning of the meal as the key ingredient in Sesame Tofu, served in a handmade pottery bowl and topped with a delicate sauce and a dab of fresh green *wasabi* (Japanese horseradish). The setting is bound to be exquisite: a low table arranged on raised tatami mats next to a pine-shaded pond perhaps, or a room adjoining a Japanese garden of raked white sand and a few carefully placed rugged stones. The beauty and serenity create a timeless world where the heart and mind grow still and the natural flavors can be deeply enjoyed.

For the tea master and his guest, kudzu powder appears in *Kaiseki Ryori*, a light meal that precedes the formal tea ceremony and is considered to represent Japan's haute cuisine. Here kudzu powder is used to lend delicate flavor inconspicuously and give subtle body to a clear, hot broth, while holding a few slices of carefully cut vegetables in an artistic pattern. It may also be found in a single cube of Walnut Tofu, or served as a light sauce over wild vegetables in season.

For the hot and weary traveler, in the late spring or early summer, kudzu powder appears in a refreshing dessert called Fresh Kudzu Noodles in Molasses Sauce (*Kudzu-kiri*). At Kagizen, a centuries-old restaurant in Kyoto, tall and elegant multilayered containers are brought to thick wooden tables by women in traditional dress. Remove the monogrammed lid, and in a small bowl one finds a cool, fragrant sauce. Lift away this tier, and deep in the second black lacquerware hollow are long, flat, opalescent strips of jelled kudzu looking like hand-cut noodles and intertwined with large chunks of ice beneath a faint, chilled mist. Pluck them out with hardwood chopsticks, dip them into the sweet sauce — and the heat of summer is soon forgotten.

For the devotee of traditional Japanese confectionery (*o-kashi*), kudzu powder appears throughout the summer in a great variety of forms served in specialty shops, temples, or wayside inns with new spring tea or ceremonial *matcha* (whisked green tea). One very popular confection is Kudzu-zakura, consisting of a spoonful of deep-red, sweet *azuki* bean paste enfolded in a soft, translucent coating of jelled kudzu and served on a delicately perfumed cherry leaf reminiscent of Mount Yoshino's thousand cherry trees. Kudzu Mochi, another favorite, is a bite-sized mound of jelled kudzu sprinkled with a layer of *kinako* (roasted soy flour) and a little natural sweetening.

For the priest in his mountain hermitage or temple, the family who enjoys foraging for edible wild plants, or the farmer who lives off the land from time to time in order to make ends meet, the kudzu vine offers its leaves, shoots, flowers, seeds, and roots for use in a variety of preparations such as tempura, pressed salads, sautéed vegetables, or pickles.

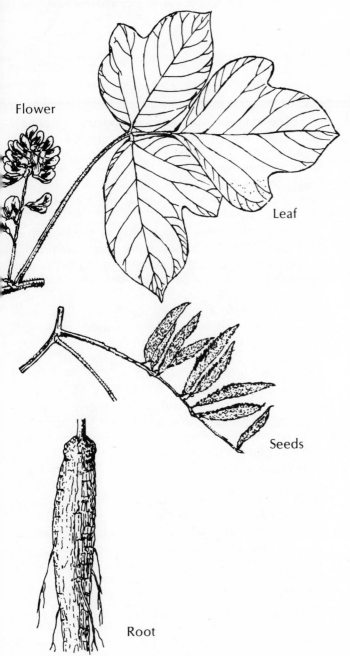

Flower

Leaf

Seeds

Root

For the doctor, healer, or invalid who wishes to rely on effective traditional remedies, kudzu powder is made into a smooth and soothing thickened broth called Kudzu Cream (*Kudzu-yu*), which helps to develop an alkaline constitution. It also provides quick relief from intestinal and digestive disorders (particularly upset stomach and acid indigestion), hangover, fever, colds, and a variety of more serious ailments. Small dried cubes of the unprocessed kudzu root (called *kakkon*) have long been used in traditional herbal medicine (*kanpoyaku*) as the key ingredient in the medicinal mixture called Kakkonto. And chlorophyll extracted from kudzu leaves is used commercially on a large scale or mixed with enzymes and sold in small quantities at some Japanese health food stores.

For the weaver, young kudzu vines harvested in their first year, shortly before the first killing frosts, provide supple waterproof fibers known in the West as kohemp, superior in quality to Manila hemp, linen, nettle fiber, or sisal, and having 80 percent of sisal's tensile strength. Extracted from the vines by hand, using a traditional, natural process, these long, silky fibers are prized for their almost translucent luster and the ease with which they take natural dyes. Folk weavers from Shizuoka and Miyagi Prefectures use these fibers to make a lovely and highly durable cloth called *kappu*, which is, in turn, fashioned into the stylish *katsui* ("kudzu kimono") or occasionally used for everyday clothing or rainwear. Kudzu kimonos made by Kyotos' master weaver, Tsugio Odani, are highly prized and sell for more than $400.

Kakkon   Kappu   Katsui   Tsuzura kago

For the maker of fine traditional paper, the cellulose fiber from large, crushed kudzu vines and roots serves as the basic raw material. For the back-to-nature fisherman, the pliant fibers offer a readymade line. And for the basket maker, the flexible young vines become the sturdy wicker baskets or trunks known as *tsuzura kago*. (Notice that four of the italicized words mentioned above began with the same character, meaning "kudzu"; each, however, is pronounced differently.)

For the country builder or homemaker, short sections of kudzu fiber (generally discarded during the extraction of the root starch) serve as a reinforcing agent in Japanese-style plaster walls prepared by mixing the fibers with mud and clay. Kudzu fiber is also used as a stuffing for cushions, beds, and chairs; when burned, it acts as a mosquito repellent.

For the rural farm family, kudzu's leaves and green seeds serve as a plentiful, easily harvested source of nutritious, protein- and chlorophyll-rich livestock fodder, or as an excellent mulch, green manure, or compost base. And for the beekeeper, kudzu thickets provide a source of unusually fragrant, flavorful honey.

For the conservationist and aesthete alike, cultivated kudzu vines cover mile after mile of steep embankments along roadways and railway lines the entire length of Japan. Unlike the ugly (and expensive) concrete embankments used in the West, the kudzu plant, with its colorful greenery, enriches the scenery, while its elaborate root system holds the earth in place, preventing landslides, and its fast-growing vines blanket the ground, checking topsoil erosion and adding layers of rich humus to the soil with their fallen leaves.

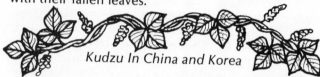

Kudzu In China and Korea

Kudzu is said to have originated in China (whence it was taken to Japan); it has been a part of Chinese culture for over two millennia. There it is called either *ko* or *ko-shu* (the Chinese character for *ko* is identical to the Japanese character for *kudzu*, and the character for *shu* means "belonging to the class of"). The Chinese value the kudzu plant primarily for its diced, dried root (called *ko-kên*), which serves as the key ingredient in the widely used and highly esteemed medicinal Kudzu Root Tea and has been employed since earliest times to treat influenza, fever, dysentery, and even snake and insect bites. Kudzu powder (called *ko-fên*) and kudzu flowers are also used to a limited extent in both medicine and cuisine, especially the Buddhist vegetarian type. The cloth made from the vine fiber, known as *ko-pu* (literally, "kudzu cloth") or *kung-pu* ("offeratory cloth"), is both durable and light, and is highly prized for summertime use.

In Korea, kudzu is now widely cultivated. The vine fibers are used to make kudzu grasscloth, which a rapidly expanding industry exports throughout the world. Starch from the roots is exported to Japan in semi-refined form and used domestically to make kudzu powder.

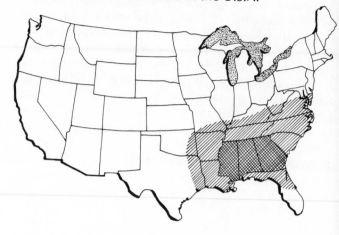

Distribution of kudzu in the U.S.A.

Kudzu in America

The tempestuous history of kudzu in America is so bizarre that it is sometimes referred to as a "cosmic joke." Kudzu was first brought to the United States from Japan in 1876: it was grown in the Japanese pavilion at the Philadelphia Centennial Exposition. It appeared again at the New Orleans Exposition of 1883.

In the first stage of its history in America, from 1876 until 1910, kudzu was used as an ornamental shade plant. It gained popularity for its decorative dense foliage, which provided welcome shade on sweltering summer days and could be used by gardeners to create a shielding background (to block out the view of neighboring houses) or a lush tropical effect. It was also appreciated for its attractive fragrant flowers and for the fact that it grew quickly in almost any type of soil. In 1902 David Fairchild, author of *The World Was My Garden*, planted a number of kudzu seedlings around his Washington, D.C., home and found that they "all took root with a vengeance, grew over the bushes and climbed the pines, smothering them with a mass of vegetation which bent them to the ground and became an awful tangled nuisance." He tried for years to eradicate the vine, but with only limited success. His caveat did not appear in print until 1938; meanwhile, people all over the South were planting kudzu along their porches and arbors, having propagated it either by crowns or seeds, which became increasingly available in mail-order catalogs.

The second stage, from 1910 to 1935, saw the development of kudzu's use as livestock pasturage, fodder, and hay. Fairchild, while serving in Japan as a plant explorer for the U.S. Department of Agriculture, had noticed that wild kudzu was used as pasturage, and had started the plants in Washington, D.C., partially to test them for this purpose. Further preparation for this stage began in 1902 when a farmer in the Florida panhandle town of Chipley, Mr. C. E. Pleas, who was apparently unfamiliar with Fairchild's work, became disappointed with the poor performance of his ornamental kudzu; so he yanked it up and replanted it near a garbage pile behind his house. Nothing can match the fury of a spurned kudzu plant, and within two years that pile and much of the area around it were smothered by the luxuriant vine and had never looked so good. However, it was only after Pleas noticed that his chickens, cows, goats, pigs, and horses all liked to eat the leaves that he began to have an inkling of the plant's potential. Believing that he had stumbled on a discovery that would usher in a prosperous new era, Pleas set out with messianic zeal as the first promoter of kudzu cultivation. By 1910 he had devoted 35 acres to kudzu pasturage and was selling fodder by the wagonload. In 1925 he wrote a pamphlet entitled *Kudzu — Coming Forage of the South*; meanwhile, he promoted the plant through the mails and sold root cuttings from which new vines could be started. The U.S. Post Office Department once investigated Pleas for mail fraud. The investigating officer simply did not believe that any plant could grow as fast as Pleas said kudzu would, but after visiting Pleas's farm for several days, he dropped the investigation with apologies. Pleas spent forty years of his life at his kudzu crusade; he died in 1954, disappointed by growing criticism of kudzu but still convinced of its virtues. After Pleas's death a bronze marker was erected on U.S. 90, near his local agricultural center, announcing that "Kudzu Was Developed Here." The message explains that Pleas developed this "soil-saving, high-protein plant." Workers at the center report that "people driving down here from Georgia see the marker and stop, just so they can come in and cuss us."

As early as 1907, kudzu hay had appeared at an exhibition in Jamestown, Virginia, and by 1917 the Alabama Agricultural Experiment Station at Auburn had begun to study kudzu's fodder value. In 1920 John Rigdon, pioneer conservationist from Columbus, Georgia, and agricultural agent for the Central of Georgia Railroad learned of kudzu's remarkable growing speed and excellent nutritional value; he convinced the railroad that the prolific plant, sold as fodder, could provide them with extra freight to haul. And before long, the railroad had initiated a vast program to provide free plants and advice on how to grow kudzu for animal feed. Most southern agriculturalists, however, still viewed kudzu cautiously. The general feeling was that "Its

value would be primarily as a permanent pasturage on lands too rough or too poor to till." Thus, by 1934, only about 10,000 acres had been planted in kudzu throughout the South.

The third stage of kudzu's history in America, from 1935 to 1955, saw the plant burst into prominence in soil conservation programs throughout the South. By 1935 the South's soil and agrarian economy were suffering from terminal malnutrition; the farmers were as poor as their worn-out land, which had been depleted by decades of careless and intensive planting in cotton, tobacco, and corn. Farmers deserted their sterile farms in droves; abandoned ditches grew into gulleys, until eventually the red clay of the eroded countryside was covered with huge running sores. Only a miracle, it was believed, could save dear old dying Dixie.

But the growing number of kudzu crusaders felt they had just the answer, and careful experiments reconfirmed their hunch: not only did kudzu grow on hard, scarred land devoid of topsoil, it flourished—in fact, it even revitalized the soil by giving back nitrogen-rich nutrients. Moreover, its deep roots let it laugh at drought.

The reign of kudzu began in earnest when the various agricultural agencies that sprang up during FDR's New Deal joined forces with the crusaders. In 1933 Congress established the Soil Erosion Service, which in 1935 became the Soil Conservation Service (SCS), whose main function was to keep the South from washing away. Among the various plants that were tested as potential cover crops, kudzu looked like the one that could do the job. As early as 1935, the SCS began recommending kudzu for erosion control; by 1936 it was growing the vine on thousands of acres of demonstration plots and using plants specially imported from Japan as one of the key measures for erosion control on Tennessee Valley Authority dam projects. But the response of southern farmers was still cool; they were aware of kudzu's aggressive growth pattern and feared that widespread planting might result in its uncontrollable spread and the loss of entire farms. Even some SCS technicians hesitated to advocate the use of kudzu except in controlling isolated gullies. Nevertheless, while its initial image was not entirely favorable, additional experimentation and intensive promotion changed kudzu's fortunes. Careful tests conducted at southern agricultural experiment stations during the twenty years prior to 1936 began to show conclusively that kudzu was, in fact, remarkably effective in checking erosion (especially in terrain so gullied that other plants could not grow), replenishing soil nutrients, and providing pasturage and hay. This combination of scientifically demonstrated properties gave the vine noteworthy credentials, which gradually caused the farmers' fears to subside. Consequently, the SCS embarked on a massive planting campaign. The U.S. Department of Agriculture and state agricultural extension services published bulletins extolling kudzu's virtues and outlining the procedures for its successful establishment. To encourage farmers to plant it as a conservation measure, the government offered assistance payments running as high as $8.00 per acre. By 1940 SCS nurseries had produced over 73 million seedlings, some of which were started with seeds imported from Japan. From Maryland to Texas, and especially in Georgia, Alabama, and Mississippi, thousands of workers from the Civilian Conservation Corps were employed to plant kudzu along highways and byways, and in every gulley and gorge. Hugh H. Bennet, head of the SCS, fueled the growing enthusiasm for kudzu when he lauded the fast-growing ground cover thus:

> What, short of a miracle, can you call this plant? Kudzu has forced our Service to revise our appraisal of a lot of severely eroded land as having been ruined for further agricultural use. And it is not only a good crop for gouged-out land; it is a splendid crop for good land too. It will cover a cornfield in one year; the next spring or early summer it can be plowed and the land planted to corn; then after the last cultivation of the corn it will again spread over the field, stop erosion, store more nitrogen, and at the first hard frost lay down a carpet of rich leaf litter at least the equal of forest litter. All this in one year.

Japanese crest, stylized kudzu leaf and flower

By the late 1930s kudzu had been introduced into every southern state and was reaching the height of its popularity. In 1939 the first comprehensive (thirty-page) booklet about the new plant was written by R. Y. "Kudzu" Bailey, the SCS regional agronomist at Spartanburg, South Carolina, and one of kudzu's greatest proponents. Even Japanese agriculturists got caught up in the growing fervor: after returning from a visit to the southeastern United States, Mr. Mukaeda Toshio wrote a sixty-four-page booklet, the title of which translates as "Kudzu: The Plant to Save Japan." In 1945 Readers Digest

published "Kudzu: Another Agricultural Miracle" by Russell Lord (a consultant to the USDA), thereby introducing the plant and the new word to people across the nation.

One of kudzu's most famous and ardent supporters was Channing Cope, widely identified as the "father of kudzu" because he constantly wrote about it in the Atlanta Constitution and broadcast its virtues from his front porch radio program. A fat, jovial man who always wore a floppy straw hat and an enormous grin, Cope used kudzu to transform his own 700-acre Yellow River Farm (located southeast of Atlanta) from a piece of eroded, worn-out land into a verdant pasture on which he grazed beef cattle. By the late 1930s, when Cope started actively promoting kudzu, it was already the rage in agricultural circles; he merely joined the stampede. In 1943, capitalizing on the fad, he formed the Atlanta-based Kudzu Club of America, which soon had over twenty thousand card-carrying members; they held rallies, zealously spread the kudzu gospel, and eagerly planted the vine in every nook and cranny. Georgia even held beauty contests to elect its annual "Kudzu Queen." Some people closely connected with the SCS identified with the plant so strongly that they adopted its name; they started calling themselves, for example, "Kudzu" Smith or "Kudzu" Cole. No religious movement is complete without a bible, and by 1949 Cope had finished writing one, Front Porch Farmer, which sold over eighty thousand copies and thrust him briefly into national prominence. His theory, based in part on his own farming success, was amazingly simple yet devilishly appealing. Each farmer, Cope proposed, should have some kudzu and other green pasturage growing somewhere at all times. Then all the farmer would have to do is nudge the cattle from one field to the next as the seasons changed. With reference to the eroded South, Cope noted that the Chinese had long ago ignored the potential of their native kudzu and the result had been the Gobi Desert! A lot of kudzu was planted by farmers who had read Cope's book and thought they had found an easy way to make a living and save their land. Newsweek and Time interviewed him, and soon the merry agricultural tinkerer came to be known as "The Prophet." In a moment of crowning insight, he joyously cried out the lines that have since become famous: "Cotton isn't king here anymore. Kudzu is king!"

By 1945 it was estimated that kudzu was growing on approximately 500,000 acres in the Southeast. Local residents had come to call it the "miracle vine." By 1948 the acreage in Georgia alone had mushroomed to 480,000 acres and Cope's Kudzu Club set as its goal 1 million acres in Georgia and 8 million acres for the South as a whole by 1950. The vine had become one of the most favored domesticated plants in the South, and attitudes toward it approached reverence. Many people felt that kudzu played a key role in helping the South in its hour of need. As one spokesman has put it: "Why, the whole state of Georgia would have washed down into the Atlantic Ocean if kudzu hadn't reached out, grabbed hold of all that dirt, and held it back!"

The fourth stage in kudzu's tempestuous and comical history began in about 1955, when the very people who had promoted the miracle vine so fervently started to become disenchanted with it. As one southerner wrote: "It was like discovering Ole Blue was a chicken killer." Kudzu now turned on its masters. Once declared the savior of the South, it gradually came to be considered at best a nuisance, at worst a scourge. In some areas the rapacious ravager was declared a "national disaster," and as kudzu overleaped its bounds and started marching through Dixie, some people began to panic. In 1976, on the one hundredth anniversary of kudzu in America, newspaper headlines boldly announced: "The South is fighting another war ... and losing once again."

Japanese crest, stylized kudzu flower

James Dickey has called kudzu "a vegetal form of cancer"; he sees it as "evidence of the tremendous power of life to go on, maybe senselessly, maybe divinely ... beautifully ... maybe uselessly." Together with killer bees and Japanese honeysuckle, it has come to be viewed as part of the ecological exotica of the South.

Why has kudzu spread so rapidly? First, the South's combination of a long growing season, a warm climate, and plentiful rainfall create a uniquely favorable environment for kudzu's growth. Second, in America the plant has almost no natural enemies. (In Japan, by contrast, a less ideal environment plus insect predators and disease keep the vine in check.) And finally, the momentum of its initial propagation here was hard to slow down. Measurements have shown that under ideal conditions, kudzu can grow 1 foot a day and up to 100 feet in a season. Channing Cope once calculated that a single acre of kudzu, left uncontrolled for a hundred years, would expand to 13,000 acres.

Throughout the early 1950s, the growing disenchantment with kudzu led to a steady decline in newly planted acreage. Under the Agricultural Conservation Program, for example, 36,000 acres were planted in 1947, but only 8,000 acres in 1951 and 3,000 acres in 1953. The visionary goal of the Kudzu Club was never to be met. In 1954, when the Department of Agriculture removed kudzu from its list of acceptable cover crops, the plant began a quick slide into ignominy. And during the 1960s, the focus of research shifted from cultivation to eradication. Although kudzu may still appear to be spreading, statistics show that total acreage has actually decreased, largely as a result of restrictions in planting, plus eradication programs. The 1970 estimate of 85,000 acres is a mere 17 percent of the estimated maximum of 500,000 acres attained between 1945 and 1950. Nevertheless, in forests and other areas where kudzu is hard to control, it is now spreading rapidly. And the remaining acreage is still large, with much of it in areas where the plant is highly visible and troublesome.

Why has kudzu declined in favor? Basically because too much was expected of the plant, and its negative aspects, initially glossed over, began to stand out as southern farming moved into the modern era.

The lumber industry and U.S. Forest Service are kudzu's strongest critics today, because it has been playing havoc with timber production in the South, especially in recent years, as more southern acreage was turned to forests. Kudzu invades whole forests, climbing saplings and even 100-foot-tall trees, patiently smothering them by cutting off necessary sunlight with its dense foliage. Each year hundreds of thousands of dollars' worth of good lumber and pulpwood are lost to its onslaught. Moreover, kudzu can prevent the establishment of new forests by completely covering the ground.

Telephone companies reportedly have trouble with kudzu pulling down poles; occasionally they have been forced to run their lines underground. In Dickey's words:

> ... Far Eastern vines
> Run from the clay banks they are
> Supposed to keep from eroding,
> Up telephone poles
> Which rear, half out of leafage,
> As though they would shriek,
> like things smothered by their own
> Green, mindless, unkillable ghosts.

Power companies must spray the plants at least once a year to prevent them from sending tentacles sometimes as much as 80 feet up high voltage towers, where they can short out transmission lines and transformers, causing expensive damage. Highway department crews use herbicides and mowers in their daily skirmishes to try to prevent the plant from covering road signs and guardrails or running out on shoulders and bridges; its spread keeps the sun off the pavement and holds in moisture, which deteriorates concrete. Railroaders also battle kudzu; they tell of how the vines can grow across the tracks on grades and be churned into a slimy mush under a locomotive's wheels, causing them to slip and the train to stall. Consequently, railroads and highway departments had begun to eradicate the plant along their rights of way as early as the 1950s, and today it is no longer used for bank stabilization except in areas that will support no other plants.

Farmers dislike kudzu most when it sneaks onto their property and damages crops and fruit trees, while providing an unwanted haven for green snakes. It is still widely used as pasturage for grazing livestock, but care must be taken to prevent over-grazing, which can eventually kill the plant. Its leaves provide a nutritious hay, but kudzu's woody stems, accounting for over one-half the hay crop by weight, have little nutritional value and make it difficult to cut and rake without special equipment. Kudzu is still considered excellent for erosion control, but recent years have seen the development of perennial grasses (such as fescue, coastal bermuda, bahia, and lespedeza) that are better for both forage and soil stabilization, hardier, more productive, and much less troublesome. They can be planted and harvested with ease and do not race through fields and woods, smothering valuable plants and trees.

It was perhaps only natural that as kudzu fell from favor, it became the brunt of an almost endless stream of southern humor. Among southern rural folk, it came to be known as the "mile-a-minute vine" or the "foot-a-night vine"; kudzu and bamboo were said to be the only two things that grow so fast you can measure growth in miles per hour. An Arkansas farmer once quipped that, "When you plant kudzu, drop it and run." One legend tells of a man who planted kudzu behind his barn, and its branches grew fast enough to beat him back to the house. Another asserts that the tale of *Jack and the Beanstalk* was but a slightly exaggerated account of a boy who was careless with kudzu. In some rural areas children are warned that if they are naughty they will be thrown into the kudzu patch and swallowed up. Stories are told of how a kudzu vine once climbed a tree, reached down, grabbed a well cover, and then yanked it into the air. In Georgia, legend says that you must close your windows at night to keep kudzu from coming into the house.

Kudzu grows so fast, it can cover an abandoned car in a few weeks and completely engulf an empty house in the course of a summer, growing in one side and out the other. "The stuff will smother anything," says Ed Laws, head of Georgia highway maintenance. "It'll even smother you if you stand around long enough." The story is told of the drunken farm hand whose last embrace was in the hairy arms of kudzu; or of the aviator who had the misfortune to land his stricken craft in a kudzu patch and was discovered only years later. When a group of northern tourists visiting Georgia recently were awed by its lush greenery and asked an agricultural official if kudzu could be transplanted to their state, they were invited to take home as many truckloads as they wanted, but warned that they would be better off taking home a rattlesnake.

In Marjie Short's hilarious film *Kudzu* (see appendix C), a paunchy southern farmer, asked what he thinks about kudzu, looks squarely into the camera and, speaking in a slow, determined southern drawl, replies: "Well, there's three things I really hate: first is kudzu, second is city life, and third is mosquitoes. 'Cause all of 'em works just about hand in hand in making your life miserable—especially kudzu." He then goes on to propose that the United States government, instead of sending its precious grain to Russia, send kudzu seeds instead!

Tifton B. Merritt, a southern journalist, gives the following advice for cultivating kudzu:

Choosing a plot: Although kudzu will grow quite well on cement, you should select an area having at least a little dirt.

When to plant: Kudzu should be planted at night to avoid neighbors seeing you and throwing rocks.

Fertilization: Forty-weight, nondetergent motor oil applied to the underside of tender leaves prevents their scraping when kudzu begins its rapid growth.

Mulching: For best results, as soon as the young shoots begin to appear, mulch heavily with concrete blocks!

Japanese crest, stylized kudzu leaves

Like it or not, kudzu has become as much a part of the South as Mardi Gras and mint juleps. It has inspired poetry and song, and starred in movies. A southern rock band calls itself Kudzu and sings

"Talkin' 'bout the Kudzu Vine." A now defunct underground newspaper in Birmingham, Alabama, was named *Kudzu*, and a circle of Atlanta writers, the Channing Cope Memorial Journalism Cooperative, has as its motto: "Covers Dixie like the Kudzu." A group of kudzu krazies have made a film entitled *Kurse of the Kudzu Kreature*, which tells the moving tale of how the kudzu goddess wreaks her vengeance on an infidel who violates her sacred grotto.

Japanese crest, stylized kudzu leaves

Kudzu's Future

In the United States, there are two schools of thought about what should be done with kudzu. The first school, comprising most southerners, advocates eradication. The problem is, nobody has yet found a practical way to stop it. You can poison the vegetable medusa with any of a number of newly developed, highly toxic herbicides (see chapter 6), but this method is very expensive and hard on the environment, and repeated applications are required over several years. It also kills all nearby plants and makes the land unfit for growing other crops for six to twelve months; exposed to the elements, the large areas of land on which no other crops will grow are subject to severe erosion. Moreover, for safety reasons, the government is banning some of the poisons that work best. A simpler way to eradicate kudzu is to allow cattle to overgraze it. Unfortunately, however, cattle do not climb trees, where kudzu does its most pernicious work. Rufus Adair of Georgia's *Elberton Star* has proposed leaking a story that kudzu is hallucinogenic. "The hippies and the government would be racing to see who could get it first," he says wryly. One woman urged in a recent *Atlanta Constitution* editorial that the federal government pay the unemployed to dig up kudzu (however, that might start a dangerous forty-year cycle of planting and removing the vine at the taxpayer's expense).

The second school feels that we should start using kudzu creatively instead of complaining about it or trying to kill it. Granted, kudzu now has an image problem and is suffering from a bad press, but that can always be changed. In their carefully researched "Rise and Decline of the 'Miracle Vine' Kudzu in the Southern Landscape," John Winberry and David Jones conclude that kudzu's greatest value for the future lies in its unique ability to solve three specific soil erosion problems: control of newly cut channels, stabilization of steep road cuts, and coverage of mine spoils and denuded areas that will support no other plants. In recognition of kudzu's potential contribution in these problem areas, the SCS began in 1971 its first seedling production in nineteen years: a limited number of plants are now being produced in Americus, Georgia, and the search is on for a prolific seed-bearing strain.

With the rise of modern chemical agriculture and advanced Western technology, kudzu's key roles have been replaced by more up-to-date and convenient equivalents: chemical fertilizers, soy-and-grain fodders, concrete embankments. Yet Dr. Jake Tinga, a horticulturist with the University of Georgia Agriculture College experiment station, notes that "With the costs of fossil fuel, fertilizer, irrigation systems, and other agribusiness necessities steadily going up and up, farmers may start to re-examine some less sophisticated, less expensive methods of production. If properly managed, kudzu may yet have a place in agriculture." As a starter, he suggests planting the vine in barrels on the roofs of new buildings and letting it cover the structure to serve as a natural coolant, helping to reduce air-conditioning costs.

In the same vein, kudzu is beginning to attract interest among the present generation of Americans interested in living self-sufficiently, closer to the land and in greater harmony with it. Once again its leaves are being used to mulch organic gardens, enrich compost piles, and fatten livestock, leaving corn, soybeans, wheat, and oats for human consumption.

Researchers at Vanderbilt University in Tennessee are investigating the use of the vines and leaves for fuel and the use of the root as a fermentation substrate for the production of both baker's yeast and ethanol fuel. Preliminary experiments indicate that the abundant root starch can easily be converted to reducing sugars containing alpha-amylase and glucoselike substances. Moreover, they have found that the root seems to provide all the vitamins needed for a very nutritious food and support for yeast fermentation.

We believe, however, that kudzu's greater future in America lies in the use of the root as a source of the remarkable kudzu powder and the medicinal kudzu root. Information about kudzu's culinary and healing properties was first introduced to the West during the 1960s by teachers of Oriental philosophy and medicine such as Georges Ohsawa,

Michio Kushi, Noboru Muramoto, and Herman Aihara. Amazingly, in the extensive kudzu literature produced by Americans during the past century there is not a single reference to these uses so famous throughout the Orient. Yet today a growing number of Americans are using kudzu in the ways described above—and respect for its virtues is steadily increasing. How fruitful, indeed, is the meeting of East and West!

Let us hope that the coming years will mark the inception of a fifth phase in kudzu's American odyssey. Already work is underway in a number of diverse areas to relate to kudzu in new and creative ways:

1. Kudzu powder is now being used in lieu of lower-quality cooking starches and is featured in some of America's finest natural food restaurants. We may soon even witness the rise of a new southern delicacy, kudzu candy!

2. Kudzu Root Tea and Kudzu Creams are being used by naturopaths and appearing in their books on healing.

3. As imports of the handsome kudzu grass-cloth wallpaper steadily increase, Americans may want to look more carefully into the possibilities of producing it domestically. The modern processes used for extracting fiber from flax might well be applied to kudzu.

4. Organic farmers in northern states are experimenting with planting kudzu. (In the colder, dryer climate growth can be kept under control.)

5. Several people have shown interest in starting the first commercial kudzu shops in the West to supply high-quality, natural powder and root at domestic prices.

Before long, the South may come to be viewed as a treasure trove bursting with "white gold" just waiting to be harvested. When this day arrives, kudzu will have found its true home in America—this time for real.

2. Cooking with Kudzu

WHETHER IT is used to thicken sauces or soups, to add a light and crispy coating to deep-fried dishes, to give form and gentle softness to pudding-like preparations, or jell a variety of wonderful confections and treats, kudzu powder can make your favorite Western-style dishes—and a wide variety of Japanese-style preparations—even more healthful and delicious. The leaves, shoots, flowers, and roots of the kudzu plant also provide a number of tasty dishes.

In each category (sauces, soups, etc.), we have listed our *favorite recipes first*, and we suggest that you begin with them.

Basic Principles

By learning the basic proportions of kudzu powder and liquid needed to produce different thickening and jelling consistencies, you can begin to experiment more freely with using kudzu in your favorite recipes:

Preparation	Liquid	Kudzu Powder
Clear soups	1 cup	½ to ¾ teaspoon
Beverages	1 cup	¾ to 1 teaspoon
Thin sauces or Western-style soups	1 cup	2 teaspoons
Medicinal creams or *ankaké* sauces	1 cup	1 tablespoon
Thick sauces	1 cup	1½ to 2¼ table-spoons
Jelled liquids and glazes	1 cup	2 tablespoons
Tofu-like jelled preparations	1 cup	2¼ to 2½ table-spoons
Fresh kudzu noodles	1 cup	4 tablespoons
Kudzu Mochi	1 cup	5½ tablespoons

Kudzu powder may be substituted for flour, arrowroot, or cornstarch as a thickening agent in most recipes. Use the following proportions:

1 teaspoon kudzu powder = 3 teaspoons flour
1½ teaspoons kudzu powder = 3 teaspoons arrowroot
4½ teaspoons kudzu powder = 3 teaspoons cornstarch

Acidic liquids such as lemon juice require 10 to 15 percent more kudzu powder for thickening or jelling than water or alkaline liquids such as apple juice.

Most of the recipes in this book call for the use of at least one of the following preparatory techniques:

Dissolving Kudzu Powder: Combine the powder and cold liquid in a small bowl or cup. Stir well, then mash any remaining lumps with fingertips. Pour through a small, fine-mesh strainer into cooking liquid, retrieving all kudzu from bowl with a rubber spatula. Dip strainer in cooking liquid to rinse.

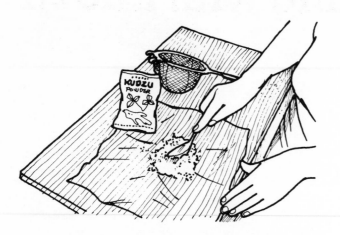

Crushing and Sifting Kudzu Powder: Place chunky powder on a piece of plastic wrap, paper, or foil, and crush with the back of a large spoon. (Or crush large amounts with a wooden pestle in a *suribachi* or mortar; clean grooves of the former with a dry brush when finished.) Sift and rub through a fine-mesh strainer.

For greater ease and accuracy in measuring kudzu powder, crush and sift the chunks before using measuring spoons. For larger quantities, or when sifting is not convenient, use a scale: 1 cup of powder weighs about 7 ounces (175 grams), and 1 tablespoon about ½ ounce (11 grams).

It is helpful to keep the following points in mind when cooking with kudzu powder:

1. Always dissolve the powder thoroughly in cold liquid (usually water) before heating it or adding it to a hot dish.

2. Stir continuously with a wooden spoon when cooking.

3. Heat the dissolved powder over a medium flame until you feel it begin to thicken; then turn the flame down to low.

4. Continue stirring, scraping the entire surface of the bottom of the pan to prevent sticking, lumping, or burning.

5. Within 1 to 2 minutes after the milky liquid has begun to thicken, it will suddenly become transparent. Generally the mixture is then stirred vigorously for about 1 more minute and finally removed from the fire. However, in the case of firmly jelled dishes such as Sesame Tofu or Peanut Tofu, the mixture is usually stirred for as long as 10 to 15 minutes over low heat in order to develop a uniquely smooth, resilient texture.

6. Prevent jelled kudzu powder from sticking to fingers and molds by moistening them with water.

Kudzu powder is used in Japanese cookery for many of the same purposes for which we in the West use arrowroot, cornstarch, or gelatin, and for which the Japanese use agar and the various starches made from Irish potatoes, sweet potatoes, wheat, and bracken ferns. However, kudzu is fundamentally different from these other products in the flavor and texture it imparts to foods, in the traditional natural method used in its preparation, and in its basic alkalinity (the others are all acidic). Real kudzu powder (as contrasted with the less expensive imitations described in appendix B) now retails for about 25 to 30 cents (U.S.) per ounce in Japan and 40 to 50 cents in the United States. Although it is much costlier than the other starches, connoisseurs agree it is worth the price.

The arrowroot plant

Arrowroot has long been a favorite among natural-food fanciers because it is processed by rather simple traditional methods, without the use of bleaches or other chemicals, and produces a delicate texture and appealing flavor surpassed only by kudzu. Although it has no known medicinal properties, this fine-grained, pure-white starch is highly digestible, thus excellent for use in the diets of invalids and children. Almost the entire world supply of arrowroot comes from the island of St. Vincent in the West Indies. The arrowroot plant (*Maranta arundinacea*), a tropical perennial with swollen, starchy rhizomes, is propagated by planting the rhizomes and digging them up about ten months later. They are then peeled, washed, grated, and sifted repeatedly in order to extract the starch, which is finally dried. In the West this starch is used primarily as a thickening rather than a jelling agent, especially in puddings and pie fillings. A bargain at about 21 percent the retail price of kudzu powder per unit weight, arrowroot nevertheless lacks kudzu's alkalizing and medicinal value. To create an equal-strength jell, twice as much arrowroot as kudzu must be used, and the resultant product has a slightly undesirable "starchy" flavor and a milky color. Moreover, it lacks firm cohesiveness and will weaken further if it is allowed to stand at room temperature.

Cornstarch is America's most widely used cooking starch, largely because of its low retail price (about 37 cents per pound, or 6 percent the price of kudzu powder). Unlike arrowroot and kudzu powder, cornstarch is not a whole food, since the life-giving germ of the corn kernels is removed before wet milling; this process results in a longer shelf life but a loss of flavor and vital nutrients. During milling, the starch is heavily processed with complex equipment in huge factories and treated with bleaches and extractive chemicals. To create an equal-strength jell, only two-thirds as much cornstarch as kudzu powder is required, but the resultant product is overly elastic and has a slightly brownish color and a flavor that masks the flavors of the jelled ingredients.

Gelatin is derived from collagen, the prime constituent of all white fibrous connecting tissue in the bodies of animals. About 90 percent of the commercial product is made from animal hide stock and the remainder from ossein (bone protein matrix). In order to make gelatin, the hides, skins, sinews, and crushed bones are treated with acid or alkali and boiled in water for a long time. After the grease has been skimmed off, the solution is cooled, dried, and ground to a powder. Gelatin's greatest drawbacks are that it melts at room temperature and will not jell acidic liquids having a pH of less than 4.5.

Agar

Agar (also called kanten or agar-agar) is a traditional natural jelling agent prepared from the sea vegetables *Gelidium* and *Gracilaria*. Sold as flakes, light-as-air bars, or powder, agar keeps jelled foods firm yet delicate in the very hottest weather and jells even acidic pineapple juice. Agar makes excellent jams and jellies without the addition of sugar or honey (unlike pectin, so widely used in the West, which requires considerable sweetening). Discovered in Japan in 1647 and long a favorite among vegetarians, agar is prepared by boiling the dried plants, jelling the filtered liquid in molds, freezing it (traditionally outdoors in the mountains on winter nights), then thawing and drying it repeatedly to make the finished bars, which may also be crumbled to yield flakes. The powder is generally prepared using a large-scale, modern industrial process.

Potato Starch (*bareisho denpun*) is Japan's foremost domestically produced starch. Generally marketed as *katakuri-ko* (an ancient term referring to starch from the root of the dog-tooth violet, a wildflower that closely resembles the Western "shooting star"), the product is processed by quick chemical methods in large modern factories and retails in Japan for about 32 cents per pound.

Sweet-potato Starch (*kansho denpun* or *Satsuma denpun*) is Japan's second most widely produced domestic starch. Its price is slightly higher than that of potato starch, but its flavor and texture are said to be superior. It is used more by the food industry than in private households.

Table 1. Composition of Nutrients in 100 Grams of Edible Starches.
Sources: *Standard Tables of Food Composition* (Japan), *FAO Food Composition Tables*, and *USDA Composition of Foods* (Washington, D.C.)

Food	Food Energy	Moisture	Protein	Fat	Carbohydrates Sugars	Fiber	Ash	Calcium	Sodium	Phosphorus	Iron
	(Calories)	(%)	(%)	(%)	(%)	(%)	(%)	(Mg.)	(Mg.)	(Mg.)	(Mg.)
Kudzu Powder	336	16.5	0.2	0.1	83.1	0	0.1	17	2	10	2.0
Kudzu Root, Dried	—	13.6	13.3	2.2	32.1	31.4	7.4	—	—	—	—
Sweet-Potato Starch	336	16.5	0.1	0.1	83.2	0	0.1	35	2	18	2.0
Cornstarch	362	12.0	0.3	0.1	87.6	0.1	0.1	0	0	0	0

* Dashes indicate unknown quantities: though kudzu powder and root have been found to be rich in vitamins, exact figures have not yet been published.

Wheat Starch (shofu) is extracted like corn-starch and is used widely in Japan for jelled confections, particularly Kudzu Mochi.

Bracken Starch (warabi denpun), extracted from the root of the bracken fern, is mostly used in Japan to make the popular confection called Warabi Mochi, which is prepared and served in much the same way as Kudzu Mochi.

Although there is a world of difference between the flavors and textures of kudzu powder and other starches, their nutrients are actually quite similar, as shown in table 1.

Despite its high cost and relative rarity, kudzu powder is preferred by many discerning confectionery shops, restaurants, and households throughout Japan for five basic reasons:

1. *Flavor:* Kudzu's subtle flavor and unique aroma enhance rather than interfere with the delicate flavors of its companion foods, and it adds no starch overtones. The potato starches, by comparison, have a slightly "green" or "raw" taste.

2. *Texture:* Although it has excellent jell strength, kudzu powder results in jelled products that are usually described as soft, smooth, and gentle on the tongue; they readily surrender their firmness and form to melt in the mouth. The potato and corn starches are considerably more elastic, or "chewy." Not only is less kudzu powder generally required to bring jelled and thickened dishes to the proper consistency, its smooth, even grain enables it to retain its form and flavor for a long time, even at warm temperatures. (This quality can be enhanced by the addition of agar.)

3. *Translucency:* When simmered for several minutes or thoroughly steamed, kudzu powder imparts sparkling clarity and subtle luster to sauces, soups, and jelled desserts. Other starches cannot be made to attain this degree of translucency, which is particularly prized in Japanese jelled confections. When cooked, kudzu's starch molecules are converted from their basic "beta" form into the radiant "alpha"; unlike other starch molecules, they stay in this form for as long as 2 to 3 days without becoming opaque or losing jell strength.

4. *Crispness:* When vegetables or tofu are dusted with sifted kudzu powder just before deep-frying, they emerge with a uniquely crisp and delicately crunchy golden-brown coating, which cannot be matched by even the best arrowroot or cornstarch. The Japanese call this coating *koromo* ("priest's robes"). Even if dusted foods are allowed to cool before being served, they retain this spindrift delicacy.

5. *Alkalinity:* Because of its unique biochemical alkalinity, kudzu powder can be used to balance small amounts of sweetening (which are acidic) to yield a delicious variety of treats and confections that leave the body feeling light and the mind alert. Kudzu's presence in any recipe not only guarantees the healthfulness of that dish, in many cases it turns food into medicine.

The combination of these factors, the Japanese have found, makes possible subtle harmonies and overtones of flavor, texture, and appearance that can make the difference between a taste experience that is merely enjoyable and one that is exquisite.

Basic Recipes

The preparations in this short section, although they contain no kudzu, are used in a number of the recipes in the following sections. Japanese ingredients are described in the Glossary; most are readily available at Japanese food markets and many natural food stores in the West.

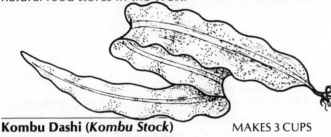

Kombu Dashi (*Kombu Stock*)   MAKES 3 CUPS

1 strip of *kombu*, 3 by 7 inches
3 cups water

Wipe kombu lightly with a moistened, well-wrung cloth, then combine with the water in a small saucepan and bring just to a boil. Turn off heat, remove kombu, and reserve for use in other cooking.

Number 1 Dashi (*Ichiban Dashi*)   MAKES 3 CUPS

This preparation is a cornerstone of Japanese cooking. For best flavor, use bonita flakes which have been shaved just before use. An instant dried *dashi* (dashi-no-moto) is now widely available in the West.

3 cups water or Kombu Dashi
¼ to 1 cup bonita flakes (15 to 30 grams)

Heat the water until quite hot in a small saucepan. Add bonita flakes and bring to a boil. Turn off heat and allow to stand for 3 minutes, or until flakes settle; skim off foam. Filter the dashi through a (cloth-lined) strainer placed over a saucepan. Press flakes with the back of a spoon to extract remaining dashi, then reserve flakes for use in other cooking.

Shoyu-Wasabi Topping   SERVES 1

1 teaspoon natural soy sauce (shoyu)
¼ teaspoon *wasabi* (Japanese horseradish)

Pour soy sauce over preparation to be served, then top with a dab of wasabi. (Note: Freshly grated wasabi is more delicious, but powdered wasabi—which is mixed with water just before use—is more readily available and less expensive.)

Rich Shoyu Sauce   SERVES 6 TO 8

5 tablespoons dashi, stock, or water
2 tablespoons natural soy sauce (shoyu)
2 teaspoons honey
1 teaspoon sake or white wine
2 teaspoons wasabi (grated or powdered)

Combine the first four ingredients in a saucepan and bring to a boil. Reduce heat to low and simmer for 1 minute. Cover and set aside to cool, or refrigerate. Use with wasabi.

Wasabi

Sweet Miso Topping
SERVES 8

5 tablespoons red, barley, or *Hatcho* miso
1½ teaspoons *mirin*
2 tablespoons honey
1½ teaspoons sake or white wine
¼ cup dashi, stock, or water

Combine all ingredients in a small saucepan and simmer, stirring constantly, until mixture becomes almost as thick as the original miso. Set aside to cool. When refrigerated, portions will last indefinitely.

Packaged tofu

Creamy Tofu Dressing
MAKES 1 CUP

6 ounces tofu, well drained
1½ tablespoons lemon juice or vinegar
2 tablespoons oil
¼ teaspoon salt
1 teaspoon natural soy sauce (shoyu) or 1½ teaspoons red miso; or substitute ¼ teaspoon salt
Seasoning (choose one)
    4 to 6 fresh basil leaves
    ¼ teaspoon dill seeds and, if desired, 1 clove of minced garlic
    2 tablespoons minced onion and ½ teaspoon curry powder

Combine the first five ingredients and the seasoning in a blender; purée until smooth. Serve topped, if desired, with a sprinkling of parsley.

For *Tofu Mayonnaise*, omit the soy sauce and seasoning; use ½ teaspoon salt and, if desired, a dash of pepper.

Tofu Whipped Cream
MAKES ¾ CUP

6 ounces tofu
1 to 2 tablespoons honey
¼ teaspoon vanilla extract (optional)
Dash of salt (optional)

Combine all ingredients in a blender and purée until smooth. Serve chilled.

Grain Coffee (*Yannoh*)
SERVES 10 TO 20

Yannoh is a nutritious, caffeine-free coffee made from five different grains and beans. Available prepackaged at many natural food outlets, it can also be prepared at home.

3 tablespoons brown rice
2 tablespoons whole wheat
2 tablespoons *azuki* beans
1 tablespoon garbanzo beans (chickpeas)
1 tablespoon chicory
1 tablespoon oil

Roast the first five ingredients separately in a heavy skillet until well browned. Heat oil in an empty skillet, add roasted ingredients, and sauté for about 3 minutes, or until fragrant. Allow to cool, then grind to a powder in a suribachi or purée in a blender. For serving instructions, see Kudzu-thickened Beverages.

Tempura Dipping Sauce
SERVES 4 TO 6

1 cup dashi, stock, or water
3 to 4 tablespoons mirin, sake, or pale dry sherry
¼ cup natural soy sauce (shoyu)
4 to 6 tablespoons grated *daikon*
4 to 6 teaspoons grated gingerroot

Combine the dashi, mirin, and soy sauce in a small pan. Bring just to a boil over high heat, then set aside to cool. Divide the dipping sauce, grated daikon, and grated gingerroot among 4 to 6 small serving bowls and serve with deep-fried preparations.

Natural Japanese soy sauce

Sauces

Kudzu powder may be used in place of arrowroot, cornstarch, or katakuriko in virtually all thickened sauces; it greatly improves the texture and flavor. With noodles or simmered (or steamed vegetables), the use of the cooking liquid as the basis for the kudzu sauce adds both flavor and nutrition. Thin kudzu powder in a little water and add to the remaining liquid. Season sauce with soy sauce, miso, or salt, and, if desired, a little honey. Simmer for 1 to 2 minutes, stirring constantly, until sauce is thick and clear.

over hot, cold, or deep-fried regular or buckwheat noodles.

Lotus root

VARIATIONS

* **Other Vegetables:** Japanese chefs often use lotus root, daikon, Chinese (or regular) cabbage, *kabu* turnips, mushrooms, beansprouts, or cauliflower in place of the vegetables listed above.

* **Delicate Kudzu, Shoyu & Vegetable Sauce:** Sauté the vegetables as above, then add 1 cup stock or water, 5 teaspoons soy sauce, and 1½ teaspoons honey. Proceed as above but omit gingerroot; thicken with 2½ to 3 teaspoons kudzu powder dissolved in 1½ tablespoons water.

Kudzu, Shoyu & Vegetable Sauce (*Ankaké*)

SERVES 3 TO 4

1 tablespoon oil
½ onion, thinly sliced or slivered
1 green pepper, thinly sliced or slivered
½ carrot, thinly sliced or slivered
⅔ cup water, stock, or dashi
3 tablespoons natural soy sauce (shoyu)
1 tablespoon honey
1 to 1½ tablespoons kudzu powder, dissolved in 2 tablespoons water
2 teaspoons grated gingerroot or 3½ teaspoons powdered ginger

Heat a skillet or wok and coat with the oil. Add the onion, green pepper, and carrot, and sauté for about 5 minutes, or until vegetables are tender. Add the next three ingredients and bring to a boil. Stir in the dissolved kudzu and gingerroot, and simmer, stirring constantly, for about 1 minute, or until kudzu is transparent and well thickened. Delicious served

Kudzu & Shoyu Sauce

MAKES 1¼ CUPS

1 cup stock, water, or dashi
5 teaspoons natural soy sauce (shoyu)
1½ teaspoons honey
2 teaspoons kudzu powder, dissolved in 1½ tablespoons water
½ teaspoon grated lemon rind or gingerroot (optional)

Combine the first three ingredients in a small saucepan and bring to a boil. Stir in dissolved kudzu and, if used, the lemon rind, and cook for about 1 minute, or until thick. Delicious served over tofu (regular or deep-fried), fresh vegetables (particularly cucumbers), or cooked vegetables (such as daikon, bamboo shoots, squash, or *kabocha* pumpkin).

For a milder sauce, use 1 cup stock, 3½ to 4 teaspoons soy sauce, ½ teaspoon honey or 2 teaspoons mirin, and 1 to 3 teaspoons kudzu powder. Omit lemon rind.

Kudzu, Shoyu, & Gingerroot Sauce

MAKES 1¾ CUPS

1 cup stock, water, or dashi
¼ cup natural soy sauce (shoyu)
3 to 4 teaspoons honey
1 tablespoon kudzu powder, dissolved in 4 table-
    spoons water
1 tablespoon grated (or powdered) gingerroot
Dash of (7-spice) red pepper or Tabasco sauce

Combine the first three ingredients in a saucepan and bring to a boil. Stir in dissolved kudzu, return to the boil, and simmer for about 1 minute, or until transparent and thick. Mix in grated gingerroot and season with red pepper. Serve as for Kudzu & Shoyu Sauce.

Kudzu Sweet and Sour Sauce

MAKES 1¼ CUPS

1 tablespoon oil
½ onion, thinly sliced
½ small carrot, cut into irregular pieces
1 green pepper, cut into irregular pieces
¾ cup water, stock, or dashi
2 tablespoons natural soy sauce (shoyu)
4 teaspoons honey
2 teaspoons (rice) vinegar
1½ teaspoons kudzu powder, dissolved in 1½
    tablespoons water

Heat a skillet or wok and coat with the oil. Add onion, carrot, and green pepper, and sauté for 3 to 4 minutes, or until onion is transparent. Add the next four ingredients, bring to a boil, and simmer for 3 minutes. Stir in dissolved kudzu and cook for 1 minute more, or until thick.

For variety, omit the oil and vegetables; add 1 teaspoon grated gingerroot and 1 tablespoon sake or white wine to the remaining ingredients.

Kudzu-thickened Shoyu Sauce

SERVES 4

¾ cup stock, water, or dashi
¼ cup natural soy sauce (shoyu)
3 tablespoons honey
5 teaspoons kudzu powder, dissolved in ¼ cup water
1 teaspoon grated wasabi

Combine the first four ingredients in a small sauce-pan and bring to a boil. Reduce heat and simmer, stirring constantly, until transparent and quite thick. Cover and set aside to cool, or refrigerate. Pour over individual servings of regular tofu or Special Tofu (Recipe Index) and top with a dab of wasabi.

Fried Eggplants with Kudzu & Sesame Sauce

SERVES 3

3 tablespoons oil
3 small (4-inch-long Japanese) eggplants, cut length-
    wise into halves, with skin cut in a cross-hatch
    pattern
1 teaspoon kudzu powder, dissolved in 1 tablespoon
    water
½ cup water
1 tablespoon red, barley, or Hatcho miso, creamed
    with 1 tablespoon water
1 teaspoon sesame butter
Dash of powdered or fresh grated gingerroot

Heat a skillet and coat with the oil. Add eggplants and sauté for 3 minutes on each side, or until lightly browned. Arrange on individual serving plates.

Combine dissolved kudzu and ½ cup water in a small saucepan, bring to a boil, and simmer, stirring constantly, for about 1 minute, or until transparent. Mix in remaining ingredients and cook for about 30 seconds more. Serve over eggplants.

This sauce is also good with steamed or boiled broccoli, cauliflower, asparagus, or potatoes.

Fried Eggplant with Kudzu & Salt Plum Sauce

SERVES 2

1 tablespoon oil
1 large Japanese eggplant, or ½ American eggplant,
    cut into ½-inch-thick rounds
1 teaspoon kudzu powder, dissolved in 1 tablespoon
    water
½ cup water
1 large salt plum (*umeboshi*), pitted and minced
1 tablespoon natural soy sauce (shoyu)
¼ teaspoon grated gingerroot or ½ teaspoon
    powdered ginger

Heat a skillet and coat with the oil. Add eggplant and fry over low heat for 5 minutes on each side, or until lightly browned.

While frying eggplant, combine the next three ingredients in a small saucepan, bring to a boil, and simmer, stirring constantly, for about 1 minute, or until transparent. Mix in remaining ingredients and cook for about 30 seconds more. Arrange eggplants on individual serving plates and top with the hot sauce.

For variety, top with a sprinkling of ground roasted sesame seeds. This dish is also deliciously sweet when chilled. The sauce is excellent served over buckwheat noodles.

Kudzu & Pineapple Dessert Sauce MAKES 2 CUPS

1½ tablespoons kudzu powder
1 tablespoon honey (optional)
2 cups unsweetened pineapple juice
1 tablespoon lemon juice
¼ teaspoon ground nutmeg

Combine kudzu powder, honey (if desired), and ¼ cup pineapple juice in a saucepan, mix well, then stir in remaining pineapple juice. Bring to a boil and simmer, stirring constantly, for 1 minute, or until thick and smooth. Stir in lemon juice and nutmeg. Serve hot or cold over fruits (bananas, peaches), puddings, dumplings, or jelled desserts.

Kudzu-Sesame-Miso Gravy SERVES 6

1½ cups stock, water, or dashi
2 tablespoons natural soy sauce (shoyu)
2 tablespoons sweet white miso or 1 tablespoon red miso
1 tablespoon sesame butter or *tahini*
1 tablespoon honey
¼ to ½ teaspoon grated or powdered gingerroot (optional)
1½ to 2 tablespoons kudzu powder, dissolved in 3 tablespoons water

Combine the first five (or six) ingredients in a saucepan and bring to a boil. Add dissolved kudzu and return to the boil. Simmer, stirring constantly, for 2 minutes, or until nicely thickened. Delicious served over sautéed vegetables (zucchini, eggplant, cabbage), brown rice, or noodles.

For variety, add 2 to 4 tablespoons minced sautéed onions or 1 teaspoon sesame oil together with the initial ingredients.

Mock Cheese Sauce MAKES 3 CUPS

1 cup Good Tasting Nutritional Yeast
¼ cup kudzu powder
⅓ cup (unbleached white) flour
1½ teaspoons salt
2 cups water or soymilk
¼ to ½ cup margarine, melted
2 teaspoons fresh mustard (optional)

Combine the first four ingredients in a saucepan, mixing well, then gradually stir in water to form a smooth, creamy consistency. Bring to a boil over low heat and simmer, stirring constantly, for 5 to 10 minutes, or until nicely thickened. Whip in margarine and, if desired, mustard. Serve hot or cold in lieu of dairy cheese sauces.

Gingerroot

Vegetable Sauce with Kudzu SERVES 4 TO 6

The basic principles described in this recipe can be applied when sautéing a wide variety of vegatables; other favorites include bamboo shoots, daikon, turnips, burdock, and cabbage.

2 tablespoons oil (1 tablespoon may be sesame)
1 clove of garlic, crushed or minced
1 small onion, diced
1 pound zucchini, cut into pieces 3 inches long and ¼ inch square
1 cup stock, water, or dashi
1 tablespoon natural soy sauce (shoyu)
½ teaspoon grated or 1 teaspoon powdered gingerroot (optional)
1 tablespoon kudzu powder, dissolved in ¼ cup water

Heat a skillet and coat with the oil. Add garlic and sauté for 30 seconds. Add onion and sauté for 1 minute more. Add zucchini and sauté for 4 more minutes, or until barely tender. Stir in remaining ingredients and bring to a boil. Simmer for 1 minute, or until nicely thickened. Serve hot or chilled.

Savory Kudzu-thickened Tamari MAKES ½ CUP

In Nagoya and other parts of central Japan, this recipe is popular for use as a dipping sauce for *sashimi* (raw fish). Real tamari is generally used in place of soy sauce (shoyu).

1 teaspoon (sesame) oil
¼ cup natural soy sauce (shoyu)
¼ cup water
1½ teaspoons kudzu powder, dissolved in 2 tablespoons water

Heat a small saucepan and coat with the oil. Add soy sauce and bring to a boil. Add water and dissolved kudzu, and return to the boil. Simmer, stirring constantly, for 2 minutes, or until nicely thickened. Serve in small quantities over fresh or cooked vegetables or tofu.

For variety, add ½ teaspoon grated gingerroot together with the kudzu.

Soups

In Japan, kudzu powder is widely used to provide a delicate body to the popular jewellike clear soups (osumashi), and occasionally to give added substance to the ever-present miso soup. Try it also in your favorite consommé or other Western-style clear soups.

Fragrant Kudzu-thickened Clear Soup

SERVES 2

1½ cups dashi
1 teaspoon natural soy sauce (shoyu)
½ teaspoon salt
½ teaspoon sake or mirin (optional)
¾ teaspoon kudzu powder, dissolved in 1 tablespoon water
6 ounces tofu, drained and cut into 1½-inch cubes
½ leek or 2 scallions, cut into thin rounds
4 slivers of lemon (or citron) peel

Bring the dashi just to a boil over moderate heat. Reduce heat to low, add the next four ingredients and cook, stirring constantly, until soup begins to thicken. Add tofu and simmer until center of tofu is well heated. Remove tofu carefully with a slotted spoon and divide among two soup bowls. Garnish with sliced leeks and lemon peel, then carefully pour in the simmering broth. Serve immediately.

Egg and Onion Miso Soup

SERVES 2

1 cup dashi, stock, or water
¼ onion, thinly sliced
2 tablespoons green peas or 8 snow peas
1½ tablespoons red, barley, or Hatcho miso
1 teaspoon sake or white wine
1 egg, lightly beaten
½ to ¾ teaspoon kudzu powder, dissolved in 1 tablespoon water

Combine the first three ingredients in a saucepan, bring to a boil, and simmer for 5 minutes. Stir in the miso (creamed in a little of the hot broth), then add sake. Stir broth slowly in a spiral and add egg a little at a time; gently mix in dissolved kudzu, and remove from heat. Serve immediately.

Corn Soup with Kudzu

SERVES 4

1 tablespoon oil
1 small onion, minced
1½ cups fresh corn kernels
2 cups stock, water, or dashi
½ teaspoon salt
4 teaspoons kudzu powder, dissolved in ¼ cup water
1½ tablespoons natural soy sauce (shoyu)
Slivered toasted nori (optional)

Heat a large saucepan or pot and coat with the oil. Add onion and sauté for 5 minutes. Add the next three ingredients, bring to a boil, and simmer over low heat, stirring occasionally, for 15 minutes, or until corn is tender. Mix in dissolved kudzu and soy sauce, and simmer for 1 minute more, or until nicely thickened. For best flavor, refrigerate for 6 to 8 hours while flavors marry. Serve hot or cold, topped, if desired, with a sprinkling of nori.

Vegetable & Tofu Soup (Kudzu-hiki)

SERVES 3

1½ tablespoons oil
½ celery stalk, diced
½ carrot, diced
4 mushrooms, thinly sliced
2 cups dashi, stock, or water
1 teaspoon grated gingerroot
1 to 1½ tablespoons natural soy sauce (shoyu)
¼ teaspoon salt
1½ teaspoons kudzu powder, dissolved in 2 table-
    spoons water
6 ounces tofu, cut into ½-inch cubes

Heat a large saucepan or pot and coat with the oil.
Add celery, carrot, and mushrooms, and sauté for 3
minutes; remove from heat. Combine dashi, gingerroot, soy sauce, and salt in a small saucepan. Bring
mixture to a boil, then stir in dissolved kudzu. Add
cooked vegetables and tofu and return just to the
boil. Serve immediately.

Jelled Salads

Relatives of the molded salads or aspics made with gelatin, these attractive preparations make use of two jelling agents: agar provides the basic firmness and keeps the salads jelled at room temperature (which is not possible with gelatin); kudzu powder adds its prized opalescence while imparting to the salads a softer and more delicate texture.

Fresh Fruit Jelled Salad SERVES 3 to 4

1½ cups orange juice
¼ cup agar flakes
2 tablespoons kudzu powder, dissolved in ¼ cup (cold) orange juice
1 pear, apple, or banana, diced
6 diced strawberries
½ cup grapes or diced pineapple, melon, or apricots
1 tablespoon lemon juice (optional)

Combine the first two ingredients in a saucepan and bring to a boil. Simmer, stirring occasionally, for 2 minutes. Add dissolved kudzu and return to the boil. Simmer, stirring constantly, for 1 minute more, or until transparent. Add remaining ingredients, mixing well, return just to the boil, and pour into a moistened mold. Serve chilled.

Carrot, Raisin & Walnut Jelled Salad SERVES 4 to 6

1½ cups apple juice (or lemonade)
¼ cup agar flakes
2 tablespoons kudzu powder, dissolved in ¼ cup (cold) water
½ cup grated carrot
⅓ cup raisins
⅓ cup chopped walnut meats
1 teaspoon lemon juice

Prepare as for Fresh Fruit Jelled Salad (above). (To prepare the lemonade variation, substitute an equal volume of water for the apple juice, then stir in 2 tablespoons each lemon juice and honey after the kudzu mixture has been simmered to transparency.)

Guacamole Jelled Salad SERVES 5 TO 6

1¼ cups tomato juice
¼ cup agar flakes
2 tablespoons kudzu powder, dissolved in ¼ cup (cold) tomato juice
1 large avocado, mashed
2 tablespoons lemon juice
1 small tomato, diced
2 tablespoons minced onion
1 clove of garlic, crushed or minced
2 tablespoons minced celery or green pepper (optional)

Prepare as for Fresh Fruit Jelled Salad (above). For variety, serve on a bed of lettuce and top with a dollop of Creamy Tofu Dressing (Recipe Index) and a sprinkling of minced parsley.

Jelled Gazpacho with Creamy Tofu Dressing SERVES 6

1¾ cup tomato juice
3 cloves
1 bay leaf
¼ cup agar flakes
2 tablespoons kudzu powder, dissolved in ¼ cup (cold) tomato juice
1 teaspoon lemon juice or vinegar
¼ teaspoon Tabasco sauce
¾ cup chopped celery
3 tablespoons minced parsley or celery leaves
2 tablespoons chopped onion
¼ cup chopped cucumber or green pepper
Lettuce leaves
1 cup Creamy Tofu Dressing (Recipe Index)

Combine the first four ingredients in a saucepan, bring to a boil, and simmer for 2 minutes. Stir in dissolved kudzu powder, return to the boil, and simmer, stirring constantly, for 1 minute, or until clear. Remove bay leaf and cloves, stir in the next six ingredients, and pour into a mold. Chill until firm. Serve inverted on lettuce leaves, topped with a dollop of the dressing.

Deep-Fried Preparations

The use of kudzu powder is the key to creating deep-fried foods that are as light, crisp, and delicate as they are delicious.

The most widely used vegetables for deep-frying are onions, green peppers, (kabocha) pumpkin or squash, lotus root, mushrooms, green beans, sweet or Irish potatoes, and eggplants, each cut into slices about 3/8 inch thick. Regular or deep-fried tofu cut into 1-inch cubes or slices also works well. Serve the freshly deep-fried foods immediately, topped with a sprinkling of soy sauce (shoyu), dipped in a mixture of grated daikon (or gingerroot) and soy sauce, or dipped in freshly squeezed lemon juice and then lightly salted. Creamy Tofu Dressings (Recipe Index) also make a delicious Western-style topping. Or serve with a Tempura Dipping Sauce.

The five most popular ways of deep-frying vegetables or tofu with kudzu powder include:

1. *Dusting with Kudzu Powder:* This technique works best with tofu or rather moist vegetable slices. Place about 1/3 cup crushed, sifted kudzu powder in a small bowl. Roll individual foods in powder until well coated before deep-frying in relatively hot (350°F) oil.

2. *Kudzu Powderbound Breading:* Dust foods with kudzu powder, dip in lightly beaten egg, and roll in bread crumbs or bread crumb flakes; deep-fry.

3. *Kudzu Powder and Water Batter:* Mix 4 teaspoons kudzu powder with 3 tablespoons water. Dip individual foods in this batter and deep-fry.

4. *Kudzu Powder and Egg White Batter:* Mix 2 to 3 teaspoons kudzu powder with 1 lightly beaten egg white. Dip foods and deep-fry.

5. *Kudzu Powder, Water, and Egg White Batter:* Mix 6 tablespoons kudzu powder and 1 cup water in a bowl; allow to stand for 5 to 10 minutes until kudzu settles and becomes firm. Carefully pour off water and discard. Mix egg white with kudzu to form a batter. Dip foods and deep-fry.

Deep-fried Rice Balls SERVES 3 OR 4

1 cup brown rice, washed, soaked overnight in 1½ cups water, cooked, and allowed to cool
¾ cup chopped leeks, scallions, or onions
¼ cup sesame butter, tahini, or ground roasted sesame seeds
2 tablespoons red, barley, or Hatcho miso
2 teaspoons grated gingerroot
1 clove of garlic, crushed
½ cup crushed, sifted kudzu powder (approximately)
Oil for deep-frying
Kudzu Sweet and Sour Sauce or Creamy Tofu Dressing (Recipe Index)

Combine the first six ingredients, mixing well, then shape into 1½-inch balls (about twenty). Roll balls in kudzu powder. Heat the oil to 350°F in a wok, skillet, or deep-fryer. Drop in half of the balls at a time and deep-fry until crisp and golden brown. Drain balls well and divide among individual bowls. Serve hot or cold, topped with the sauce or dressing.

Crispy Deep-fried Tofu SERVES 2

1 12-ounce cake of tofu, pressed for 1 hour between layers of cloth toweling
3 to 5 tablespoons kudzu powder, crushed and sifted
Oil for deep-frying
Natural soy sauce (shoyu)

Cut tofu into 6 rectangular pieces and roll each piece in the kudzu powder. Heat oil to 350° in a wok, skillet, or deep-fryer. Drop in tofu and deep-fry until golden brown; allow to drain. Invite each person to season his or her tofu to taste with shoyu. Or serve with lemon wedges and salt (or soy sauce) and/or garnishes such as thinly sliced leeks, grated gingerroot, grated wasabi, or grated daikon.

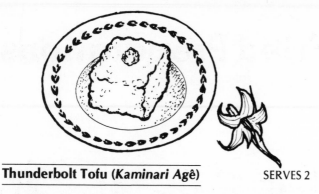

Thunderbolt Tofu (*Kaminari Agê*)　　SERVES 2

This popular recipe derives its name from the crackling sound made when the soft tofu is dropped into the hot oil.

1 12-ounce cake of tofu, cut crosswise into halves and drained on a cloth towel for 30 minutes
4 tablespoons kudzu powder, crushed and sifted
Oil for deep-frying
¾ cup dashi, stock, or water
3 tablespoons natural soy sauce (shoyu)
3 tablespoons mirin or sake
2 tablespoons grated daikon
2 tablespoons thinly sliced leeks or scallions
1 sheet of nori, cut into ⅛-inch-wide strips

Pat the tofu pieces with a dry cloth to remove surface moisture and roll them in kudzu powder. Heat oil to 350° in a wok, skillet, or deep-fryer. Drop in tofu and deep-fry until golden brown. Allow to drain, then place in deep serving bowls. Combine dashi, soy sauce, and mirin in a small saucepan and bring almost to the boil. Pour this sauce over the tofu and top each portion with grated daikon, leek slices, and nori.

Deep-fried Tofu in Dipping Sauce (*Agedashi-dofu*)　　SERVES 4

Agedashi is one of Japan's favorite deep-fried preparations. Its name is composed of two Chinese characters meaning "to deep-fry" and "to serve." What could be quicker or easier? The key to the flavor lies in the use of sesame oil, and in cutting the tofu with chopsticks (rather than with a knife) after placing it into the dipping sauce. The roughly cut surface helps the sauce's flavor to permeate the tofu.

2 12-ounce cakes of tofu, pressed for 1 hour between layers of cloth toweling
Oil for deep-frying (preferably 3 parts vegetable and 1 part sesame)
1 egg, lightly beaten
¼ to ½ cup kudzu powder, crushed and sifted
Mirin-Shoyu Dipping Sauce (*Wari-shita*):
**　　5 tablespoons dashi or stock**
**　　3 tablespoons natural soy sauce (shoyu)**
**　　2 tablespoons mirin**
2 teaspoons grated gingerroot or a mixture of 1 teaspoon each grated daikon and grated carrot
2 tablespoons minced leeks

Cut each cake of tofu lengthwise into halves, then crosswise into thirds. Pat each piece with a dry cloth. Heat oil to 350° in a wok, skillet, or deep-fryer. Dip tofu into egg, then roll in kudzu powder. Deep-fry until golden brown. Serve with the dipping sauce and garnishes.

For variety use as the dipping sauce: 5 tablespoons each soy sauce and lemon juice or vinegar.

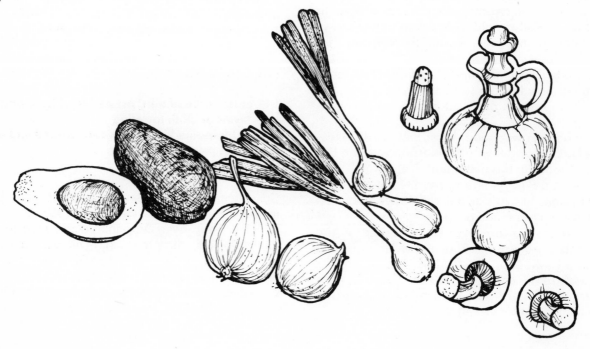

Grains with Kudzu Powder

In virtually all traditional societies, cereal grains have served as the staff of life. Even today, they are nature's most abundant and least costly food.

Noodles with Kudzu-Vegetable Sauce

SERVES 3 TO 4

We recommend buckwheat noodles (*soba*), which are most delicious homemade or purchased fresh. One key to the flavor of this recipe lies in using the noodle cooking water as the basis for the sauce.

5 cups water
3½ ounces noodles
Kudzu, Shoyu, & Vegetable Sauce, with noodle cooking water substituted for stock
1 sheet of nori (optional), toasted and slivered

In a large pot, bring water to a rolling boil over high heat. Scatter noodles slowly over surface of water and return to the boil. Lower heat until water is boiling actively and cook uncovered for about 5 to 8 minutes, or until noodles are tender but not soft. Pour noodles into a colander set over a large pot and drain briefly, then transfer to a large container filled with circulating cold water. Stir noodles for several minutes until they cool to temperature of water, then transfer back into colander set in sink; drain well. Reserve noodle cooking water in pot.

Prepare Kudzu & Shoyu Sauce, substituting noodle cooking water for stock. Sauce may be served over hot, cold, deep-fried, or fried noodles:

* Hot Noodles: While sauce is cooking, bring about 1 quart fresh water to a boil in a saucepan. Place 1 individual portion of noodles into a small strainer, dip noodle-filled strainer into boiling water for about 5 seconds, then shake strainer above saucepan to rid noodles of excess moisture. Transfer noodles to individual serving bowls, ladle on sauce, and top with slivered nori.

* Cold Noodles: Ladle on sauce and chill. Serve topped with nori.
* Deep-fried Noodles: Fill a wok, heavy skillet, or deep-fryer to a depth of 1½ to 2 inches with oil and heat to 350°F. Drop in cooked noodles and deep-fry for several minutes until crisp and golden brown. Drain briefly on absorbent paper, then serve immediately, topped with sauce and nori.
* Fried Noodles: Heat a wok or skillet and coat with 2 to 3 tablespoons oil. Add noodles and stir-fry over high heat until slightly crisp. Apportion among bowls and top with sauce and nori.

Fried Noodles with Kudzu Sauce

SERVES 4 TO 6

2 tablespoons oil
1 small onion, thinly sliced
1 small carrot, slivered
3 cabbage leaves, slivered
4 ounces buckwheat (or regular) noodles, cooked (see above) and drained
¾ cup water
2 tablespoons natural soy sauce (shoyu)
¼ teaspoon salt
1 tablespoon kudzu powder, dissolved in ¼ cup water
½ teaspoon grated, or 1 teaspoon powdered ginger-root (optional)
1 scallion, cut into thin rounds and/or ½ sheet of nori, toasted and slivered (optional)

Heat a wok or skillet and coat with the oil. Add onion and carrot, and sauté for 2 minutes. Add cabbage and sauté for 3 minutes more. Add cooked noodles and sauté for 3 more minutes (cut noodles into 3-inch lengths with spatula if desired).

Meanwhile, combine water, soy sauce, salt, and dissolved kudzu in a separate saucepan and bring to a boil. Simmer, stirring occasionally, for 1 minute, or until transparent and well thickened. Stir in ginger-root (if used), then pour this sauce into noodles in wok. Mix lightly and serve, topped (if desired) with scallions and nori.

Brown Rice Porridge with Kudzu

SERVES 2 OR 3

Called *Congee* in China and *Okayu* in Japan, rice porridge is a popular main course at breakfast in many homes and temples. Easy to digest, it is considered the ideal food for sick people. The addition of kudzu powder to the traditional recipe gives an even creamier texture and enhances the preparation's healing properties. Delicious anytime, this recipe has been used for centuries in Japan in times of famine.

½ cup brown rice, rinsed and soaked overnight in 4½ cups water
2 tablespoons kudzu powder, dissolved in ¼ cup water
Seasoning: sesame salt, sea salt, natural soy sauce (shoyu), or miso
Crumbled toasted nori and/or diced leeks (optional)

In a heavy covered pot, bring water and rice to a boil over high heat. Reduce heat to low, set lid slightly ajar, and simmer for about 90 minutes, or until rice develops a porridgelike consistency. Stir in dissolved kudzu and return to the boil. Serve immediately, seasoned to taste and topped, if desired, with nori or leeks.

VARIATION

* To Pressure Cook: Combine rinsed, unsoaked rice in a pressure cooker with 2½ cups water. Bring to pressure (15 pounds), reduce heat to very low, and simmer for 45 minutes. Remove from heat and allow to stand for 10 to 15 minutes while pressure comes down naturally. Open pot and mix porridge well. Allow to stand uncovered for 3 to 5 minutes before serving.

* With Sautéed Vegetables: About 15 minutes before porridge is ready, heat a wok or skillet and coat with 1 tablespoon (sesame) oil. Add ½ slivered carrot and 2 thinly sliced onions, and sauté for 3 minutes. Add 12 ounces tofu, mashed well, and sauté for 5 minutes more. Stir in 2½ tablespoons soy sauce and remove from heat. Add this mixture to the finished porridge, mix well, and allow to stand for 5 to 10 minutes before serving.

Primary Foods Made from Kudzu Powder

The following recipes, while delicious dishes in their own right, have been widely used in Japan and China in times of scarcity or famine. For centuries people throughout the provinces have prepared their own semiprocessed kudzu powder at home and kept a supply in reserve to be used in emergencies either as a substitute for rice or as an extender (as described in the previous section). During the more than 225 recorded famines (including the great famines, which have occurred about once every fifty years), many people are said to have stayed alive and healthy using recipes such as these. In the 1700s, the Tokugawa Shogunate actively encouraged people to make and store kudzu, and suggested delicious ways to serve it as a primary food. During World War II, these recipes once again experienced widespread popularity. If you live near a large field of kudzu and find your food supplies running low or your food bill getting out of hand, you might like to give these good old standbys a try. In each case, salt can be substituted for the salt plum and/or soy sauce.

Georges Ohsawa, founder of the international macrobiotic movement, made the following statement in his autobiography: "Our primary foods are brown rice, millet, barnyard millet and broomcorn millet [*awa*, *hie*, and *kibi*], buckwheat, and kudzu." In chapter 3 we discuss further the various ways in which Japanese naturopaths have suggested that kudzu powder be used in place of grains as the primary staple in the diet. Such a regimen is not only extremely low in calories and inexpensive (the 2 tablespoons of kudzu powder required to jell 1 cup of liquid add only 74 calories and cost $.32), it also helps to alkalize the bloodstream, which has a therapeutic effect on the entire organism. Any of the medicinal recipes given later can be used as the basis of the diet. The following are simply more substantial variations.

Jelled Kudzu Cream with Salt Plum & Shoyu

SERVES 1 OR 2

Prepare Kudzu Cream (Recipe Index) with Salt Plum & Shoyu, but increase the amount of kudzu powder to 2½ tablespoons. Pour into a cup, bowl, or mold and allow to set. Serve warm or at room temperature.

Jelled Kudzu Cream

SERVES 1 OR 2

Prepare Kudzu Cream, (Recipe Index) but increase the amount of kudzu powder to 2½ tablespoons. Pour into a cup, bowl, or mold and allow to set. Serve hot or at room temperature.

Thickened or Firm Kudzu Cream

SERVES 1 OR 2

Prepare as in the basic recipe in chapter 3. Serve as directed.

Special Tofu with Kudzu

Sesame, peanut, and walnut tofu are unsweetened, subtly flavored tofu-like treats served with traditional Japanese cuisine. Since these dishes have somewhat the same soft and delicate custard-like texture as real tofu, each bears the tofu name. They are usually served with various shoyu dipping sauces or may be topped with a dab of any of Japan's many delicious varieties of miso.

Sesame tofu, the most popular variety, is served at the beginning of the meal in most restaurants featuring Zen Temple Cookery (*shojin ryori*) and Tea Ceremony Cuisine (*kaiseki ryori*), Japan's two main types of haute cuisine. Each chef has his own unique (and often highly secret) way of preparing both the special tofu and the sauce that accompanies it. Each of these three main types of special tofu are available at large food markets and at some natural food stores in Japan. They are usually sealed in plastic containers accompanied by a separate container of dipping sauce.

Sesame Tofu (*Goma-dofu*)   SERVES 6 TO 8

In the following basic recipe, the tofu is prepared using whole roasted sesame seeds puréed in a blender. Whole seeds yield the best flavor, roasting gives the tofu a rich brown color and delicious nutlike fragrance, while the blender makes the process quick and easy. An even easier approach (described as a variation) is to use tahini or sesame butter; however, there is a slight loss in aroma. Some Japanese chefs prefer to use either unroasted or only lightly roasted sesame seeds to obtain a subtler, more delicate flavor. The seeds are generally ground by hand in a suribachi until they turn into a smooth, slightly oily paste. In shops making commercial Sesame Tofu, the seeds are ground by machine for about 5 hours to obtain the ideal consistency. The longer the tofu is stirred while thickening, the finer the texture. Commercial shops and restaurants often mix large quantities vigorously for up to 30 minutes.

6 tablespoons (white) sesame seeds
2½ cups water
5½ tablespoons kudzu powder
½ teaspoon salt
Shoyu-Wasabi Topping (Recipe Index)

Roast sesame seeds over medium heat in a heavy skillet, stirring constantly, until they are well browned and begin to pop. Place in a blender with ¼ cup water and purée for 20 to 30 seconds, gradually increasing blender's speed. Turn off blender, rinse down walls with ½ cup water, and purée again. Rinse off walls and lid of blender with 1½ cups water, add kudzu powder and salt, and purée for about 3 minutes more. Immediately pour contents of blender into a fine-mesh strainer set over a small saucepan. Using your fingertips, rub as much of the solids as possible through the strainer, then douse the sesame seed hulls left in the strainer with the remaining ¼ cup water. Again rub sesame residue against strainer. Then discard any remaining seed hulls.

Heat contents of saucepan over medium heat, stirring constantly with a wooden spoon until mixture begins to thicken. Reduce heat to low and stir for about 12 minutes more. Pour sesame mixture into a moistened metal or glass mold, preferably one with square corners and a flat bottom. (If a mold is not available, the sesame mixture may be cooled in the saucepan.) Smooth surface of mixture with moistened fingertips. Partially immerse mold in cold water and allow to cool, then cover with a sheet of plastic wrap or wax paper and refrigerate until thoroughly chilled and firm. Cut into individual portions with a moistened knife and apportion among deep (lacquerware) bowls or individual serving dishes. Serve with Shoyu-Wasabi Topping.

VARIATIONS

* Any of the following toppings may also be used:

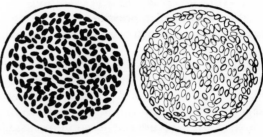

Sesame plant and seeds

Rich Shoyu Sauce, Thickened Shoyu Sauce, Sweet Miso Topping, Kudzu & Shoyu Sauce topped with a dab of grated gingerroot or hot mustard, or Kudzu-Gingerroot Sauce.

* Tahini Tofu: Substitute 4 tablespoons tahini for the whole sesame seeds in the basic recipe. Before cooking, mix all ingredients thoroughly using a spoon, egg beater, or blender. Or, for a richer version, use 2½ cups water or dashi, ½ cup tahini, 6 tablespoons kudzu powder, 2 tablespoons sake, and ½ teaspoon each salt and honey.

* Sesame Butter Tofu: Substitute 3 tablespoons sesame butter for the sesame seeds in the basic recipe. Prepare as for Tahini Tofu.

* Hand-ground Sesame Tofu: Prepared in a suribachi, this tofu has a slightly finer texture and richer flavor than that made in a blender; and the slow, almost primitive work of grinding the seeds can be most relaxing and enjoyable.

Using the same ingredients as in the basic recipe, place the hot roasted (or unroasted) seeds in a suribachi and grind with a wooden pestle for about 10 minutes, or until a smooth paste is formed. Add the water, salt, and kudzu powder, crushing the powder thoroughly with the pestle; mix well. Using your fingertips, a rubber spatula, or a small stiff brush, carefully remove as much of the ground sesame as possible from the suribachi grooves while mixing it with the other basic ingredients. Then proceed as in the basic recipe for Sesame Tofu.

* Relatives of Sesame Tofu: Use almonds, cashews, filberts, Brazil nuts, sunflower or poppy seeds, substituting 6 or 8 tablespoons of any one of these for the sesame seeds in the basic recipe.

Peanut Tofu   SERVES 4 TO 6

½ cup peanuts or 4 tablespoons peanut butter
2½ cups water
5½ tablespoons kudzu powder
¼ to ½ teaspoon salt or 2 tablespoons honey (optional)

Combine peanuts and 1 cup water in a blender and purée at high speed for about 2 minutes, or until smooth. Without turning off blender, rinse off inside walls with remaining water, add kudzu powder and purée for 30 seconds more. (If peanut butter is used, the ingredients may be mixed with a spoon rather than a blender.) Pour mixture quickly into a small saucepan and proceed as for Sesame Tofu. Serve chilled, with Shoyu-Wasabi Topping. If preparing the sweetened version, increase kudzu powder to 6 tablespoons and top with a sprinkling of shredded coconut and chopped nut meats.

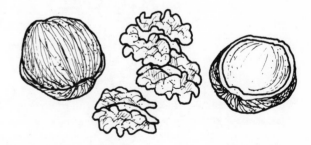

Walnut Tofu (*Kurumi-dofu*)   SERVES 4 TO 6

Follow recipe for Peanut Tofu, but substitute ½ cup chopped walnut meats for the peanuts and do not use sweetening. Serve with Shoyu-Wasabi Topping.

Emerald Tofu (*Uguisu-dofu*)

SERVES 3 TO 4

Made from fresh green soybeans, this tofu is a brilliant emerald green, as green as the *uguisu*, the Japanese nightingale.

10½ cups water
1¼ teaspoons salt
2½ to 3 cups green soybeans in their pods
5½ tablespoons kudzu powder
Kudzu-thickened Shoyu Sauce (Recipe Index)

Bring 8 cups water to a boil in a large pot and add 1 teaspoon salt. Drop in the soybeans, return to the boil, and simmer for 4 minutes. Rinse beans in a colander under cold running water; drain, and remove pods. Measure out ½ cup green soybeans, reserving any remaining beans. Combine the ½ cup beans, 2½ cups water, kudzu powder, and remaining ¼ teaspoon salt in a blender, and purée for 3 minutes, or until smooth. Pour into a saucepan and proceed as for Sesame Tofu. Serve chilled, topped with Kudzu-Shoyu Sauce.

Kinako Tofu

SERVES 4 TO 6

This recipe is the result of our experiments using kinako (full-fat roasted soy flour) to develop an easy way to make a variety of special tofu similar in flavor to Sesame Tofu but higher in protein and less expensive.

10½ tablespoons kinako
3 tablespoons oil
2½ cups water
5½ tablespoons kudzu powder
¾ teaspoon salt
Sweet Miso Topping or Shoyu-Wasabi Topping (Recipe Index)

Combine kinako and oil in a small bowl, mixing well, then stir in water, kudzu powder, and salt. Pour through a fine-mesh strainer into a saucepan. Bring just to a boil over high heat, reduce heat to medium, and cook, stirring constantly, for 3 to 4 minutes after mixture thickens. Proceed as for Sesame Tofu. Serve chilled with the topping.

For variety, prepare as for Sweet & Crunchy Seasame Tofu, but substitute the kinako and oil mixture in the above recipe for the sesame butter.

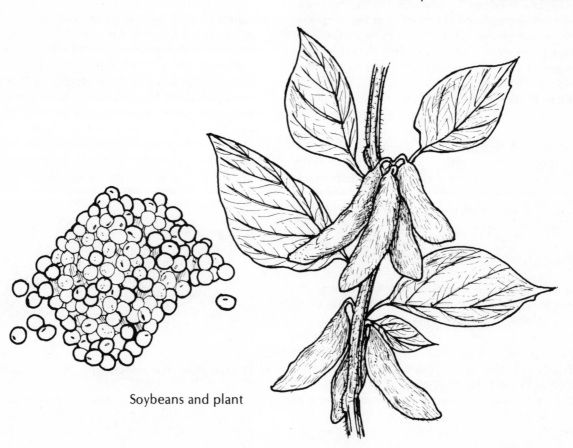

Soybeans and plant

Jelled Desserts

Many of the following recipes have a distinctively Western flair. Each is graced with a delicate texture, while the alkaline kudzu powder balances the honey to give a rich and subtle sweetness.

The combination of kudzu powder with agar, known among Japanese confectioners as *Yoshino-kan* (Yoshino is a synonym for "kudzu," and *kanten* means "agar"), gives a delicate melt-in-the-mouth consistency superior to that created by kudzu powder or agar used alone. In some pies (such as Zucchini Pie), kudzu powder can be used as a binding agent in place of eggs. In any of the following recipes, one-half of the kudzu powder may be replaced by agar in the ratio of ½ bar or 2 tablespoons of flakes for each 1 tablespoon kudzu powder. The basic method of preparation is described in the following recipe.

Kudzu & Agar Jelled Dairy Dessert   SERVES 5 OR 6

½ cup agar flakes or 1 agar bar
1 cup water
2 tablespoons kudzu powder, dissolved in ¼ cup water
1 to 2 tablespoons honey
²/₃ cup (soy or dairy) yogurt, kefir, or buttermilk
½ apple, diced or thinly sliced
3 tablespoons raisins

Combine agar and 1 cup water in a saucepan, bring to a boil, and simmer over low heat for 2 minutes, or until agar has completely dissolved. Stir in dissolved kudzu and honey, and simmer for about 1 minute more, or until kudzu is transparent. Mix in remaining ingredients, remove from heat, and pour into a moistened mold. Serve chilled.

For a simpler (yet very delicious) version of the basic recipe, omit apple and raisins; use 2 tablespoons honey.

Fruit Juice Jelled Desserts   SERVES 2

1 cup fruit juice (prune, apple, orange, or other)
2 tablespoons kudzu powder
½ teaspoon lemon juice (optional)
¼ to ½ cup yogurt (optional), chilled

Combine juice and kudzu powder in a saucepan, whisking until powder is dissolved, then bring to a boil. Simmer, stirring constantly, for 1 to 2 minutes, or until kudzu is transparent and well thickened. Pour into moistened individual cups and cool. Cover and refrigerate. Serve chilled, topped, if desired, with a sprinkling of lemon juice and a dollop of yogurt.

Jelled Buttermilk & Granola Dessert   SERVES 3

¼ cup granola
½ teaspoon lemon juice
3½ teaspoons honey
1 cup buttermilk (or kefir)
2 tablespoons kudzu powder

Mix the granola, lemon juice and ½ teaspoon honey, and use to line a small mold. Combine the remaining 1 tablespoon honey with the buttermilk and kudzu powder in a small saucepan and bring to a boil. Simmer, stirring constantly, for 1 minute, or until nicely thickened. Pour into moistened mold and allow to cool. Serve chilled.

For added richness, serve topped with Jelled Berry Glaze (Recipe Index).

Apple Pie with Kudzu-Apple Juice Glaze

SERVES 6 TO 8

This old-fashioned pie with its opalescent glaze contains no sweetener, yet has its own delicious natural sweetness and delicate texture. The glaze also does nicely atop any of your favorite fruit or vegetable pies (onion, kabocha, or pumpkin are especially good) as well as tortes and cheesecakes.

½ cup whole wheat flour
¾ cup unbleached white flour
¼ teaspoon salt
3 tablespoons (sesame) oil
⅓ cup water
½ egg white (optional)
4 (pippin) apples, thinly sliced
1⅓ cups apple juice
⅓ cup raisins
½ teaspoon cinnamon
½ teaspoon lemon juice
2 tablespoons kudzu powder

Preheat oven to 400° F. Combine flours and salt, mixing well. Add oil and rub mixture gently between palms to blend evenly. Gradually add water to form a dough and knead for 2 minutes, or just until smooth. Roll out round on a floured board and use to line a 9-inch pie plate. Flute edges, prick bottom with a fork, and brush, if desired, with egg white. Bake for 30 minutes, or until nicely browned.

While crust is baking, combine apples, ⅓ cup apple juice, and raisins in a saucepan and bring to a boil. Cover and simmer for 15 minutes. Mix in ¼ teaspoon cinnamon and lemon juice, remove from heat, and allow to cool.

While apples are simmering, combine kudzu powder and the remaining 1 cup apple juice in a small saucepan, stir until dissolved, and bring to a boil. Simmer for about 1 minute, or until transparent and nicely thickened.

Spoon cooked apples into baked crust and smooth surface. Pour kudzu glaze evenly over the top, then allow to cool to room temperature. Cover and refrigerate. Serve chilled, topped with a sprinkling of cinnamon.

VARIATIONS

* **Prune Pie:** Prepare crust as above. Simmer 2 cups (whole) prunes in 1½ cups water for 15 minutes. Cool, pit prunes, and stir in 1½ teaspoons lemon juice. Prepare glaze as above, substituting prune juice for apple juice. Proceed as above, but dot perimeter of pie with 18 walnut halves just after glaze has been poured.

* **Thickened Fruit Glazes:** With ½ cup puréed or strained fruit (apricot, peach, raspberry, strawberry, apple, or currant), combine 1 tablespoon kudzu powder dissolved in 2 tablespoons water. Bring to a boil in a small saucepan and simmer for 1 minute, or until thickened. Use as above.

Jelled Berry Glaze

FOR ONE 8-INCH CAKE

2 cups fresh strawberries, sliced; or whole blueberries
½ cup water
1½ tablespoons honey
2 tablespoons agar flakes
1 tablespoon kudzu powder, dissolved in 2 tablespoons water

Combine the first four ingredients in a saucepan and bring to a boil. Simmer uncovered, stirring frequently, for 2 minutes. Add dissolved kudzu powder and return to the boil. Simmer for 1 minute more, or until clear. Pour directly onto (hot) dessert and spread evenly with a spatula. Serve chilled. Especially delicious with Tofu Cheesecake (see *The Book of Tofu*); also good on tortes or pies.

Jelled Mulled Cider

SERVES 3 OR 4

2 cups Satin-smooth Mulled Cider (Recipe Index), cooled to room temperature
3 tablespoons agar flakes
2 tablespoons kudzu powder, dissolved in ¼ cup (cold) cider

Combine cider and agar flakes in a small saucepan, bring to a boil, and simmer for 2 minutes. Stir in dissolved kudzu, return to the boil, and simmer for 1 minute, or until transparent. Pour into a moistened bowl or mold and allow to cool to room temperature. Cover and refrigerate. Serve chilled.

Sweet & Crunchy Sesame Tofu

SERVES 3 OR 4

This Western dessert-style adaptation of the traditional Japanese favorite, Sesame Tofu, has a delightful texture and rich, hearty flavor.

3 tablespoons sesame butter or tahini
2½ cups water
6 tablespoons kudzu powder
2 tablespoons honey
½ cup raisins
⅔ cup shredded coconut
½ cup walnut meats

Combine sesame butter, water, kudzu powder, and honey in a large bowl or blender and mix or purée until smooth. Pour into a saucepan, add raisins, and cook as for Sesame Tofu (Recipe Index). Sprinkle one half the coconut over the bottom of a mold or shallow pan, and spoon in the sesame-kudzu mixture. Smooth surface of mixture, press in the walnut meats, and sprinkle on the remaining coconut. Serve chilled.

For a simpler version of the above, omit the raisins, coconut, and walnuts. Increase the amount of honey by 1½ to 3 teaspoons and, if desired, add ⅛ teaspoon salt to evoke the kudzu powder's subtle flavor and aroma.

Banana Blancmange

SERVES 4 TO 6

1 cup milk
¼ cup kudzu powder
1 banana
¼ cup water
2 tablespoons honey
1 tablespoon lemon juice
¾ cup Tofu Whipped Cream (Recipe Index)

Combine the first five ingredients in a blender and purée until smooth. Pour mixture into a small saucepan and simmer over medium heat, stirring constantly until kudzu powder begins to thicken. Reduce heat to low, and continuing to stir, cook for 2 or 3 minutes more, or until mixture becomes transparent. Mix in lemon juice, then spoon into a moistened mold partially immersed in water and allow to cool. Cover and refrigerate. Cut chilled blancmange into pieces and serve topped with the Tofu Whipped Cream.

VARIATIONS

* **Egg Blancmange:** Substitute 1 egg for the banana and prepare as above.
* **Lemon Blancmange:** Combine in a blender 1 egg,

¾ cup milk, 2 tablespoons kudzu, 2 teaspoons lemon juice, and 1 tablespoon honey. Purée until smooth then proceed as above, omitting the Tofu Whipped Cream.
* Omit Tofu Whipped Cream and serve topped with hot or cold Kudzu-Pineapple Dessert Sauce.

Powdered Green Tea Jelled Dessert

SERVES 4 TO 6

4 tablespoons agar flakes or ½ agar bar
⅔ cups water
2 tablespoons kudzu powder, dissolved in ¼ cup water
3 tablespoons honey
1 teaspoon powdered green tea (*matcha*), dissolved in 2 tablespoons water

Prepare as for Jelled Dairy Dessert (Recipe Index). For variety, omit agar and double amount of kudzu powder. Combine kudzu powder and water in a saucepan, whisking until powder is well dissolved. Bring to a boil and simmer for 1 to 2 minutes, or until kudzu is transparent and thick. Add dissolved matcha and honey, mixing well, then pour into moistened individual cups and allow to cool. Cover and refrigerate. Serve chilled.

Also delicious served with a topping of Tofu Whipped Cream (Recipe Index).

Kudzu & Calpis Jelled Dessert

SERVES 2

One of Japan's most popular and refreshing summertime drinks, *calpis* (available in most Japanese grocery stores in the United States) is a rather sweet and subtly tart fermented milk product originally developed in Mongolia. The nonalcoholic beverage, sold in bottles as a concentrate at Japanese food markets, is mixed with about ten parts water and served over ice.

2 tablespoons kudzu powder
1 cup water
2⅔ tablespoons *calpis* concentrate
¾ teaspoon lemon juice

Combine kudzu powder and water in a saucepan, whisking until powder is well dissolved. Bring to a boil and simmer for 1 to 2 minutes, or until kudzu is transparent and thick. Mix in *calpis* and lemon juice, then pour into moistened individual cups and allow to cool. Cover and refrigerate. Serve chilled.

Kudzu & Salt Plum Jelled Dessert

SERVES 2

2 tablespoons kudzu powder
1½ teaspoons honey
1 large salt plum, pitted and minced
2 teaspoons natural soy sauce (shoyu)
¾ cup water
¼ teaspoon juice squeezed from freshly grated gingerroot, or 1 to 2 teaspoons lemon juice

Combine the first five ingredients in a saucepan, whisking until kudzu powder is well dissolved. Bring to a boil and simmer, stirring constantly, for about 2 minutes, or until kudzu is transparent and well thickened. Stir in gingerroot (or lemon) juice, pour into moistened individual cups or a small bowl, and allow to cool. Serve chilled.

Azuki beans

Jelled Azuki Treat

SERVES 8

1 cup azuki beans, well rinsed and drained
2 cups water
¼ teaspoon salt
¼ cup honey
2 tablespoons kudzu powder, dissolved in ¼ cup water

Combine beans and 2 cups water in a pressure cooker and bring to full pressure (15 pounds). Reduce heat to very low and simmer for 15 minutes. Remove from heat and allow to stand for 20 minutes while pressure returns to normal. Remove lid, stir in salt and honey, and simmer uncovered for 5 minutes more. Stir in dissolved kudzu and simmer for 1 minute more until well thickened. Spoon into a moistened bowl or mold and level the surface. Set container in water to cool to room temperature, then refrigerate. Serve chilled.

Kabocha Jelled Dessert

SERVES 6

8 ounces kabocha (unpeeled), or winter squash, pumpkin, or sweet potato
¼ cup kudzu powder
1 cup water
2 tablespoons sesame butter or tahini
2 tablespoons honey
Dash of salt

Cut kabocha into 3-inch squares and boil or steam for 20 minutes, or until tender, then press through a sieve. Measure out 1 cup of this purée, reserving the remainder for use in other cookery. Combine kudzu powder and water in a saucepan, whisking until powder is well dissolved, and bring to a boil. Add kabocha purée, sesame butter, honey, and salt, and cook, stirring constantly, for about 12 minutes, or until thick. Transfer into a moistened mold and allow to cool. Serve chilled.

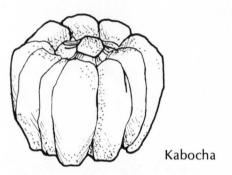

Kabocha

Kudzu-thickened Zucchini Pie

SERVES 6 TO 8

Shell for a 9-inch pie (see Apple Pie)
2½ cups cooked zucchini purée
1 cup (thick) soymilk
1½ tablespoons kudzu powder
½ cup honey
1 teaspoon cinnamon
½ teaspoon grated or powdered gingerroot

Preheat oven to 475°F. Line pie tin with shell and bake for 5 minutes. Combine zucchini purée with the remaining ingredients, mixing until smooth, then use to fill shell. Reduce oven temperature to 450°F and bake for 15 minutes. Reduce temperature to 300°F, cover edges of crust with foil to prevent burning, and bake for 45 minutes more. For the richest, sweetest flavor, serve chilled.

Japanese-Style Jelled Confections

More than 85 percent of all kudzu powder in Japan is used in the preparation of relatively sweet Japanese-style treats, especially Kudzu Mochi, Kudzu-zakura, Kudzu Manju, and Kudzu Kiri, most of which are prepared and sold at thousands of small neighborhood confectionery shops (kashi-ya). A fourth popular variety, known as Kingyoku ("Gold Jewels"), consists of a mixture of water and large amounts of sugar plus artificial coloring and/or flavoring, jelled with a mixture of kudzu powder, agar, and gelatin, and sold in interesting shapes such as: Ajisai ("Chrysanthemums"), tiny cubes of jelled kudzu attached to a flowerlike jelled hemisphere; lemon jelly half-moons, Kikko ("Turtle Shells"); and Hisago ("Gourds"). We combined the basic techniques involved in preparing these treats with natural ingredients and less sweetening to create some of the recipes in the desserts section. Interestingly, many of these foods were originally made without the use of sugar (or honey) and were considered to be natural health foods in much the same way that we in the West regard wheat germ or brewer's yeast. They were used to supplement the daily diet of grains, land-and-sea vegetables, and occasional fish or shellfish.

Many Japanese kudzu confections are made with natural sugar, which is prepared by pressing the juice from sugar cane and simmering it down to form a dark brown solid cake. Natural sugar is readily available throughout Japan in the form of large chunks known as kuro-zato (literally, "black sugar"). In the United States, however, the sale of natural sugar has long been outlawed because of pressure from the powerful refined-sugar lobbies, and virtually all of the dark sugar products here are simply mixtures of white sugar and molasses. Nevertheless, with growing nutritional awareness, a natural sugar may soon be available in America too. We feel that refined sugar is detrimental to good health and well being. In the following recipes, even natural sugar is used in the smallest amounts necessary to impart the desired subtle sweetening, and is generally balanced with highly alkaline ingredients such as kudzu powder, soy sauce, or miso. In a number of the following recipes, maple syrup may be substituted for the traditional Japanese molasses sauce.

Kudzu Mochi   SERVES 8

This is probably the most popular way of using kudzu powder in Japanese confectionery. The bite-sized pieces of jelled kudzu lightly dusted with roasted soy flour make a delectable summertime treat.

½ cup kudzu powder
2 cups water
6 tablespoons kinako (roasted soy flour)
3 tablespoons natural or brown sugar
¼ teaspoon salt

Dissolve kudzu powder in water in a small saucepan. Bring to a boil over medium heat and simmer, stirring constantly until it begins to thicken. Turn heat to low and, continuing to stir, cook for 2 to 3 minutes more, or until mixture becomes transparent and very thick. Remove from heat and allow to cool for about 20 minutes. Now, using your fingertips, break jelled kudzu into small, bite-sized pieces and arrange on a serving plate. Combine kinako, sugar, and salt, mixing well; then sprinkle over kudzu pieces. Serve chilled or as is.

VARIATIONS

* **Uji-Style Kudzu Mochi:** Add 2 teaspoons powdered green tea (matcha) to the kudzu-water mixture before cooking.
* **Kudzu Mochi with Molasses Dipping Sauce:** As soon as the kudzu has finished cooking, spoon it into a shallow pan to form a ½-inch-thick layer. Smooth surface and allow to cool to room temperature. Cut jelled kudzu into 2-inch triangles. Prepare a sauce by mixing and heating 1 part brown sugar or molasses and 3 parts water. To serve, dip kudzu triangles into chilled sauce, then roll in plain kinako.

Chinese bamboo steamer and wok

Kudzu-azuki dumplings in cherry leaves

Kudzu-Azuki Dumplings in Cherry Leaves (*Kudzu-zakura and Kudzu Manju*)

MAKES 30

Sold primarily in June and July, these popular delicacies are a feast for the eye as well as the palate; each moist, opalescent dumpling is set like a jewel in the emerald green of an individual cherry leaf wrapper. For Tokyo's *Kudzu-zakura*, a fresh cherry leaf is used; for Kyoto's *Kudzu Manju*, a fragrant cherry leaf that has been salt-pickled for one year. Both confections have the same filling.

1 cup azuki beans, washed, soaked overnight in water to cover, and drained
4¾ cups water
¾ to 1 cup natural or brown sugar
9 tablespoons kudzu powder
30 cherry leaves, fresh or pickled

Combine beans and 3 cups water in a saucepan and bring to a boil. Cover and simmer for about 50 minutes. Remove from heat and allow to cool (covered) for about 1 hour. Purée in a blender until smooth (or press through a sieve) and return to saucepan. Add salt and ¾ cup sugar, bring just to a boil over medium heat, and simmer, stirring constantly, for about 15 minutes, or until thick. Uncover and cool for about 1 hour, then shape into about thirty 1-inch-diameter balls.

Line the steaming tray of a large steamer with a moist cotton dishtowel, bring steamer to a boil, then turn heat to low.

In a small saucepan, combine kudzu powder, 1¾ cups water, and ¼ cup sugar, mixing well.

Simmer over very low heat, stirring constantly with a wooden spoon or spatula for several minutes, or until all of the milky liquid has turned to a soft white semisolid but has not yet become transparent. Remove from heat, stir vigorously for about 1 minute, then allow to cool for 1 minute. Place a large bowl of water to left of saucepan. Holding the spoon or spatula in your right hand, scoop up about 1½ tablespoons of the thick, warm kudzu. Dip your entire left hand into the water, pick the kudzu off the spatula and quickly roll kudzu into a ball and dip it into the water. Pick up a ball of azuki paste with your right hand and hold it upwards, balanced on the tips of all five fingers. Place kudzu ball atop azuki ball and, using the thumb and forefinger of your left hand, pull the soft kudzu down over the azuki ball so that all sides are completely covered. Place the covered ball upside down in your left hand and seal kudzu around ball with fingertips of right hand. Place this dumpling (seam down) in steamer. Repeat, making dumplings until all ingredients have been used. Place lid on steamer and steam dumplings for 7 to 10 minutes, or until kudzu becomes transparent. Wrap each dumpling in a cherry (or other large) leaf; cool or chill until firm before serving.

Lima Ohsawa's Kudzu Mochi

SERVES 10

1 cup kudzu powder
3 cups water
½ cup natural or brown sugar, crushed
½ cup kinako

Combine kudzu powder, water, and sugar in a small saucepan, mixing well. Bring to a boil over low heat then simmer, stirring vigorously with a wooden spoon, for 2 to 3 minutes, or until mixture thickens and becomes transparent. Spread kinako in an even thin layer on a cutting board. Pour hot kudzu mixture over kinako, spread to an even ½-inch thickness, and cut into triangular portions with a knife that has been moistened in water. Arrange triangles atop chrysanthemum or camellia leaves and serve warm or chilled.

Milk Kudzu Mochi

SERVES 4

3¼ cups milk (soy or dairy)
½ cup kudzu powder
¼ cup natural or brown sugar
¼ cup kinako (roasted soy flour)
Dash of salt (optional)

Combine milk and kudzu powder in a small saucepan and cook over medium heat, stirring constantly until mixture begins to thicken. Reduce heat to low and stir vigorously for 2 or 3 minutes, or until mixture thickens and becomes transparent. Smooth surface of mixture with a wooden spatula, then remove from stove and allow to cool thoroughly. Cut jelled mixture into small triangles or break into bite-sized pieces and arrange on four plates. Mix the sugar with enough water to form a thick syrup and pour over each serving. Mix salt with kinako and sprinkle on top before serving.

For variety, add the sugar or 2 teaspoons powdered green tea (*matcha*) to the milk together with the kudzu powder.

Other Kudzu Confections

In Japan, depending on the province and the season, the following kudzu treats and confections can also be found on sale in neighborhood confectioneries.

* Ouda-no-goko: A small square cake of dry, pressed powdered sugar filled with a mixture of mashed azuki beans, kudzu powder, kinako, powdered green tea (*matcha*), cinnamon, and ginger.

Natto (fermented soybeans)

* Sasa-no-dango: Made from *natto* (fermented soybeans) enfolded in a layer of jelled kudzu.
* Shiruko: Small, round dumplings made of jelled kudzu, sometimes served in sweet azuki bean soup.
* Kudzu Chimaki: A thin cone of jelled and sweetened kudzu, about 4 to 5 inches long and 1 inch in diameter at the base, sold wrapped in bamboo leaves.
* Mizu Botan: A treat closely resembling Kudzu-zakura but pink in color.

Thickened Beverages

Each of the following drinks has an appealing, creamy-smooth consistency and health-giving good flavor. The use of ¾ to 1 teaspoon of kudzu powder per cup of liquid gives the desired degree of thickening. Any of the medicinal creams described in chapter 3 and be made as delicious drinks by using the appropriate amount of kudzu.

Kudzu-Lemonade   SERVES 2

1 cup water
1½ teaspoons kudzu powder, dissolved in
        ¼ cup (cold) water
4 teaspoons honey
4 teaspoons lemon juice

Bring water to a boil in a small saucepan. Add kudzu powder and honey, and simmer, stirring constantly, for 1 to 2 minutes, or until kudzu is transparent and nicely thickened. Allow to cool, then cover and refrigerate. Stir in lemon juice and serve.

Satin-smooth Mulled Cider   SERVES 3

2 cups (unfiltered) apple juice
2 cinnamon sticks
6 cloves
½ teaspoon grated orange rind
1½ teaspoons kudzu powder, dissolved in
        ¼ cup (cold) apple juice

Combine the first four ingredients and bring to a boil. Add dissolved kudzu and return to the boil. Simmer, stirring constantly, for 1 minute, or until transparent. Strain if desired. Serve piping hot. Also delicious as a jelled dessert (Recipe Index).

Kudzu-Azuki Tea   MAKES 3 CUPS

This richly-flavored beverage is also valued as a natural medicine (see chapter 3).

¼ cup azuki beans
3 cups water
3 to 4 teaspoons kudzu powder, dissolved in
        2 tablespoons (cold) water
¼ teaspoon salt

Combine beans and water in a pressure cooker and bring to full pressure (15 pounds). Reduce heat to low and simmer for 15 minutes. Remove from heat and allow pressure to return to normal. Open cooker and add dissolved kudzu and salt. Bring to a boil and simmer, stirring constantly, for 1 minute, or until nicely thickened. Pour through a small strainer into individual cups; reserve beans for use in other cookery, or press through strainer and add to tea. Serve hot or cold.

For nonmedicinal usage, add 1 to 3 tablespoons honey, if desired, together with the kudzu powder; reduce salt to a pinch.

Kudzu Grain Coffee   SERVES 1 OR 2

1 tablespoon Yannoh, koko, Pero, Pionier, or other
        commercial grain coffee
1 to 2 cups water
Dash of salt
1 to 2 teaspoons kudzu powder, dissolved in
        2 tablespoons water

Combine the first three ingredients in a saucepan and simmer for 15 to 20 minutes. (For use as a medicine [see chapter 3], simmer for one full hour.) For a coffeelike consistency, strain through cheesecloth, or for a thicker consistency, serve unstrained. Add dissolved kudzu, return to the boil, and simmer, stirring constantly, for 1 minute more, or until kudzu is transparent and well thickened. Serve hot in summer or cold in winter. For variety, add a pinch of grated orange rind. A health-giving, tasty beverage.

Kudzu Dandelion Coffee

SERVES 1 OR 2

This beverage is naturally rich and deliciously sweet. Gather dandelion roots in the spring, wash and dry them thoroughly, and store sealed in a cool place; or purchase the commercial variety. Just before use, mince and dry roast over low heat in a heavy skillet. Allow to cool, then grind to a powder in a food mill or coffee grinder.

1½ teaspoons roasted dandelion-root powder
2 cups water
Dash of salt
1½ teaspoons kudzu, dissolved in
2 tablespoons water

Combine dandelion-root powder and water in a saucepan, bring to a boil, and simmer for 10 minutes or more. Add salt and dissolved kudzu, return to the boil, and simmer, stirring constantly, for 1 minute more, or until well thickened. Serve hot.

Kudzu Cream with Milk
(Kudzu-gayu)

SERVES 2

In Japan, both this and the following recipe are generally used medicinally and are sweetened with sugar rather than honey.

1 cup milk
1½ tablespoons kudzu powder, dissolved in
3 tablespoons (cold) milk
¼ teaspoon salt
1 to 2 teaspoons honey

Bring ¾ cup milk just to a boil in a small saucepan. Add dissolved kudzu and salt, return to the boil, and simmer, stirring constantly, for 5 minutes, or until nicely thickened. Remove from heat and spoon into bowls. Dissolve honey in the remaining ¼ cup milk and pour over the top. Serve warm or chilled.

Milky Chilled Kudzu (Kudzu-mizu)

SERVES 2

2 tablespoons kudzu
1 cup cold or iced water
1 tablespoon honey

Combine all ingredients, mixing well; serve chilled. Herbs (such as mint) or spices may be added to taste.

Pre-packaged kudzu beverages

Other Japanese-style Beverages Thickened with Kudzu

* Kudzu Shiruko: This and the following two recipes are famous in Shizuoka Prefecture and especially in the town of Kakegawa, where the mixed ingredients are sold in attractive paper pouches. This preparation is a mixture of cooked and sweetened powdered azuki beans (*anko*), sugar, kudzu powder, and tiny dumplings of mochi, each about ⅛ inch in diameter. To prepare, combine 3½ tablespoons with ¾ cup boiling water. Mix well and serve immediately.

* Kudzu-cha: A mixture similar to Kudzu Shiruko but with powdered green tea (*matcha*) substituted for the anko. Serve as for Kudzu Shiruko.

* Kudzu-yu: See "Modern Medicinal Preparations" chapter 3.

* Soba Tea: After cooking soba (buckwheat noodles), save the cooking water. Season with a dash of salt or soy sauce and thicken with dissolved kudzu powder.

* Mu Tea: Boil 1 to 2 tablespoons in 1 quart water for 15 to 20 minutes. Strain and thicken with dissolved kudzu powder.

* Brown Rice Tea: Roast ¼ cup brown rice until fragrant and dark brown. Add 3 cups water and bring to a boil. Simmer covered for 20 to 30 minutes. Season with salt or soy sauce and thicken with dissolved kudzu powder. Strain and serve, reserving rice for use in other cookery.

* Shiso & Salt Plum Tea: Combine 1 minced salt plum (umeboshi) and 1 teaspoon red-beefsteak-leaf juice in 1 cup water and bring to a boil. Thicken with kudzu powder.

* Roasted Barley Tea (Mugicha): Roast ¼ cup whole barley grains until dark brown (be careful not to scorch). Boil in 1 quart water for 5 to 10 minutes, then thicken with kudzu powder. Serve chilled.

Kudzu Noodles

Kudzu noodles (*kudzu-kiri*), always sold commercially in dry form, are opalescent and as slender as medium spaghetti (2 millimeters in diameter): 7-inch-long straight varieties and 15-inch-long noodles bent end to end are sold in cellophane bags; fancier types are folded in attractive swirling forms and enclosed in elegantly printed paper casings (below). In Japan, where the noodles are now widely available at natural food stores or supermarkets a typical 3½-ounce (100-gram) package costs the equivalent of $.53 U.S. cents. These ready-made products are not as yet well known or easily purchased in the United States, however, delicious Fresh Kudzu Noodles can be prepared quite easily at home.

Kudzu noodles are said to have originated in Japan during the 1200s, and since the great Zen master Dogen opened his temple at Eiheiji (about 1230), they have been used in Zen Temple Cookery. The earliest kudzu noodles were handmade. In recent years, with the rising cost of kudzu powder, makers have begun to mix in larger and larger percentages of sweet-potato starch, until at present

some varieties sold as "Kudzu Noodles" actually contain no kudzu powder at all, and the highest-quality products contain as little as 30 percent real kudzu. Due to the antiquated nature and leniency of Japanese labeling laws (see appendix A), virtually all makers avoid listing the ingredients and percentage of genuine kudzu on the package. Thus, it is almost impossible for the consumer to know what he or she is buying.

To prepare kudzu noodles commercially, real kudzu powder and potato starch are mixed in a fairly large amount of water then allowed to settle. The water is removed and discarded, and the remaining thick paste is spread in a thin layer on a metal plate and steamed (causing the beta starch molecules to change to alpha). After the steamed layer has been partially dried, it is cut (or extruded) to form noodles, which are dried either in the sun or in ovens. One company, Miwa Somen (see appendix B), makes two types of noodles in addition to kudzu-kiri; all three are almost identical in appearance and recommended usage. One variety available in America, called Kudzu Shirataki, contains 10 percent by weight of real kudzu powder and 90 percent *konnyaku* (the starch of a yamlike tuber); bleach and a binding agent are also used. The second variety,

called Kudzu Konnyaku, contains 50 percent each Korean kudzu powder and konnyaku starch. Both products are sold in 3-ounce cellophane packages and are most widely used in One-Pot Cookery (*Nabémono*).

The velvet-smooth texture and light, simple flavor of kudzu noodles makes them excellent for use in a wide variety of Western- and Eastern-style recipes. General serving suggestions include:

* **Chilled Desserts:** Top the cooked, chilled noodles with honey, maple syrup, or molasses (commercial or made by mixing dark brown sugar with water), fruit juices or wines, yogurt and fruits, and whisked green tea (matcha).
* **Salads** (Western-style or vinegared): Serve chilled noodles with fresh vegetable slices topped with your favorite dressing or a Sweetened Vinegar-Shoyu or Vinegar-Miso dressing.
* **One-Pot Cookery (Nabémono):** Cook noodles for 5 minutes, then add to *Sukiyaki* or *Mizutaki* together with your choice of vegetables.
* **Soups:** Bring noodles to a boil in the soup stock, then add remaining ingredients and cook until all are tender.
* **Chinese Cookery:** Serve like chilled Chinese noodles topped with Sweet and Sour Sauce or chilled broths.

Homemade Fresh Kudzu Noodles

SERVES 3

**6 tablespoons kudzu powder, dissolved in
   1½ cups water**

Bring dissolved kudzu powder to a boil in a small saucepan. Simmer, stirring bottom constantly with a

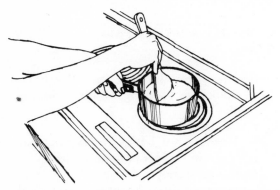

wooden spatula, for 4 to 5 minutes, or until kudzu is transparent and very thick. Spoon into a moistened 9-inch-square baking pan or dish (to a depth of ⅜-

inch) and smooth surface with a rubber spatula. Cool

quickly by setting pan in ice water, or refrigerate.

Carefully lift jelled kudzu sheet away from sides of

pan, then invert pan over a moistened cutting board. Moisten upper surface of kudzu sheet, then cut into

⅜-inch-wide noodlelike strips by pressing vertically downward with a moistened long, sharp knife (remoisten knife after each cut). Unless serving noodles immediately, transfer to a bowl of iced water. Serve as soon as possible, preferably within a few hours.

VARIATION

* The following method is used at Kyoto's famous Kagizen restaurant (see appendix B). Pour dissolved kudzu to a depth of ¼ inch into a 12-inch-diameter, flat-bottomed pan set tightly over a pot of boiling water to form a double boiler. Heat without stirring for 1 to 2 minutes until kudzu turns transparent. Immerse pan (and kudzu) in cold water, then carefully lift out jelled kudzu sheet onto a moistened cutting board. Proceed as above, and serve with Chilled Molasses Sauce (below).

Boiling Dry Kudzu Noodles   SERVES 2 TO 4

2 quarts water
1.4 ounces (40 grams) dry kudzu noodles

Bring water to a boil over high heat, in a large pot. Scatter noodles slowly over surface of water and return to the boil. Lower heat so that water is boiling actively but does not overflow. Cook uncovered for 6 to 7 minutes, or until noodles are tender. Then cover, remove from heat, and allow to stand for 6 to 7 minutes more. Drain in a colander and douse with cold running water until chilled. Makes 1¼ cups.

Fresh Kudzu Noodles in Chilled   SERVES 3
   Molasses Sauce (Kudzu-kiri)

The famed specialty of Kyoto's lovely Kagizen restaurant, this summertime treat delights both the eyes and the palate, while cooling the spirit. A similar version can be prepared with commercially available dried kudzu noodles.

⅓ cup water
5 to 6 tablespoons natural or dark brown sugar
3 servings of Homemade Kudzu Noodles (above)
6 large chunks of ice

Combine water and sugar in a small saucepan. Cook over low heat, stirring constantly, just until sugar dissolves. Allow to cool, then cover and refrigerate.

Prepare noodles. Place two large chunks of ice in each of three bowls, arrange noodles atop ice, and pour in chilled water to just cover noodles. Pour chilled molasses sauce into three separate bowls and serve together with bowls of iced noodles. Invite each guest to pluck noodles out of icewater with chopsticks or fork, then dip them into the chilled sauce.

VARIATIONS

* Substitute chilled maple syrup or honey for the molasses sauce.
* Add 1 teaspoon kudzu powder to the sauce together with the brown sugar. Bring to a boil and simmer, stirring constantly, for about 1 minute, or until transparent.

Kudzu Noodles with Sweetened   SERVES 2
   Vinegar-Shoyu

This tasty preparation closely resembles the famous Japanese recipe for *Tokoroten*, which uses agar noodles instead of kudzu noodles.

1.4 ounces (40 grams) dry kudzu noodles, boiled
   and chilled; or 2 servings Homemade Kudzu
   Noodles
Sweetened Vinegar-Shoyu
   2½ tablespoons vinegar
   2 teaspoons natural soy sauce (shoyu)
   2 teaspoons honey
½ teaspoon hot mustard
Nori, toasted and slivered

Combine chilled noodles and dressing; toss lightly. Serve in individual small bowls topped with a dab of mustard and a sprinkling of nori. Mix lightly before eating.

Kudzu Noodles with Vinegar Miso   SERVES 4
   Dressing

2.8 ounces (80 grams) dry kudzu noodles, boiled
   and chilled; or 4 servings Homemade Kudzu
   Noodles
Vinegar Miso Dressing
   2 tablespoons red, barley, or Hatcho miso
   1 tablespoon vinegar or lemon juice
   2 teaspoons honey
   ½ teaspoon mirin, sake, or wine (optional)

Combine noodles and dressing; toss lightly. Serve chilled in individual bowls.

For variety, reduce noodles to 2.1 ounces (60 grams) and cut into 2-inch lengths after boiling. Add 2 thinly sliced cucumbers before tossing. Serves 6.

Kudzu Noodles & Fruit Salad with Yogurt Dressing

SERVES 3 TO 4

1.4 ounces (40 grams) dry kudzu noodles, boiled, chilled, and cut into 2-inch lengths; or 2 servings Homemade Kudzu Noodles
1 apple, thinly sliced
1 banana, thinly sliced
Dressing
    ½ cup yogurt
    1½ teaspoons honey
⅓ cup raisins (optional)

Combine the first three ingredients with the dressing; toss lightly. Serve topped, if desired, with a sprinkling of raisins.

Kudzu Noodles & Fresh Vegetables with Sesame-Vinegar Dressing

SERVES 4

2 (*shiitaké*) mushrooms, washed
½ cup water
1 teaspoon natural soy sauce (shoyu)
1 teaspoon oil
1 egg
Dash of salt
1.4 ounces (40 grams) dry kudzu noodles, boiled and chilled; or 2 servings Homemade Kudzu Noodles
1 cup (mung) bean sprouts, parboiled
1 green pepper, parboiled and slivered
1 cucumber, slivered
Sesame-Vinegar Dressing
    2 teaspoons sesame butter
    2 teaspoons (dark) sesame oil
    1½ tablespoons vinegar
    1½ tablespoons natural soy sauce (shoyu)

Soak mushrooms in ½ cup water for 15 minutes, then drain, reserving water. Sliver mushrooms, combine with soaking water and soy sauce in a small saucepan, and bring to a boil. Simmer for 5 minutes, then drain, discarding broth. Allow mushrooms to cool.

Heat oil in a skillet, break in egg, and prepare a thin omelet. Season with salt, allow to cool, and cut into very thin strips.

Place chilled noodles in a large serving bowl. Over surface of noodles arrange sprouts, green pepper, cucumber, mushrooms, and slivered omelet, grouping each ingredient together to form a colorful design. Prepare dressing in a separate container, cover both, and chill. Invite guests to serve themselves, topping individual portions to taste with the dressing.

Kudzu Noodles with Fruit and Molasses Sauce

SERVES 4 TO 6

½ cup natural or dark brown sugar
½ cup water
1 tablespoon kudzu powder, dissolved in ¼ cup water
2.8 ounces (80 grams) dry kudzu noodles, boiled and chilled; or 4 servings Homemade Kudzu Noodles
1 banana, diced
1 cup diced melon, pear, apple, or orange

Combine sugar and water in a small saucepan and bring to a boil over low heat. Simmer until sugar just dissolves, then stir in dissolved kudzu powder and simmer for 1 minute more, or until nicely thickened. Transfer to a small serving container and allow to cool. Cover and chill.

Combine chilled noodles, banana, and other fruits in a small salad bowl; toss lightly. Invite guests to serve themselves, topping individual portions to taste with the sauce.

Kudzu Noodles & Fresh Vegetable Salad

SERVES 2 OR 3

3 large lettuce leaves
1.4 ounces (40 grams) dry kudzu noodles, boiled and chilled; or 2 servings Homemade Kudzu Noodles
1 small tomato, cut into wedges
½ cucumber, thinly sliced
Dressing
    3 tablespoons vinegar
    4 tablespoons oil
    5 teaspoons red or light-yellow miso
    ½ teaspoon powdered mustard

Line a salad bowl with lettuce leaves, add noodles, and arrange tomatoes and cucumbers on top. Spoon on the dressing.

For variety, add or substitute slivered green peppers, hard-boiled egg, green beans, or carrots. Mayonnaise dressings also work nicely.

Kudzu Leaves, Shoots, Flowers and Roots

The tender, young parts of the kudzu plant make a delicious vegetable that may be gathered wild for free. (Avoid gathering the older leaves and shoots, which are generally quite fibrous.) Wash thoroughly before use, then try serving them in your favorite salads, soups, sautéed dishes, and casseroles.

* Sautéed Kudzu Leaves: Dice young leaves fine and sauté well in oil. Serve seasoned with salt and natural soy sauce (shoyu).

* Boiled Kudzu Leaves: Boil young leaves well in water containing a pinch of salt, then soak for at least 20 minutes in cold water. Serve lightly salted or accompanied by a dipping sauce consisting of equal parts natural soy sauce and lemon juice.

* Kudzu Leaves with Sesame Dressing: Boil young leaves, wrap in a cotton dishcloth and press with several pounds weight for 10 minutes. Dice fine and dress with a mixture of 2 tablespoons tahini (or substitute sesame or peanut butter creamed with 1 teaspoon water), 1½ tablespoons vinegar, 1 teaspoon honey, and ½ teaspoon salt (or 1½ teaspoons natural soy sauce).

* Kudzu Leaves with Vinegar-Shoyu Dressing: Boil young leaves, dice fine, and dress with a mixture of 2½ tablespoons vinegar, 2 teaspoons natural soy sauce, 2 teaspoons honey, a dash of salt, and, if desired, ½ teaspoon sake or white wine and a dab of mustard.

* Deep-fried Kudzu Leaves: Dip young leaves in a thin flour-and-water tempura batter, covering both sides, and deep-fry in 350°F oil until golden brown. Serve like Vegetables Deep-fried with Kudzu.

* Fresh or Steamed Kudzu Shoots: Freshly picked young shoots may be eaten raw right in the field or taken home for use in salads; they taste like a cross between a pea and a bean. They may also be steamed and served as a vegetable side dish.

* Pickled Kudzu Greens: Use soft parts of the kudzu plant such as sprouts, buds, shoots, young leaves, and flowers. Pickle in a mixture of moistened rice bran and salt (*nukamiso*) for 1 to 3 days. Rinse and serve as a garnish for rice.

* Kudzu Flowers Pickled in Vinegar: Parboil flowers until very tender, season with the Vinegar-Shoyu Dressing described above and allow to stand for at least 1 day before serving.

* Steamed Roots: Since ancient times, kudzu roots have been used in Japan as an emergency food in times of famine. Gathered during the fall or winter, when they are rich in starch, they are cut into cubes, steamed or boiled, and served seasoned with natural soy sauce, miso, or salt.

3. Healing with Kudzu

IN JAPAN the kudzu plant has traditionally been used as a medicine in two different forms: the white powder extracted from the root is used to prepare a number of creamy beverages, such as the popular Kudzu Cream; and small tan cubes of the pulpy, dried, unprocessed root are simmered alone or with other herbs to prepare medicinal infusions known as Kudzu Root Teas.

Kuzu-ko   Kakkon

Through their strongly alkaline biochemical balance, kudzu powder and kudzu root work naturally to restore good health by alkalizing the bloodstream while combatting intestinal and digestive disorders and a host of other infirmities. In Japan they are sometimes used as nourishing health foods for invalids and the elderly. In Japanese hospitals the powder is often prescribed for patients on a liquid diet, since it is soothing, nutritious, and easy to digest.

Although the most refined, pure-white kudzu powder is generally considered to be the highest quality for use in cookery, less highly refined, slightly off-white or beige kudzu (such as that described in "Making Kudzu Powder at Home" and "Making Kudzu Powder as a Community," chapter 4) may actually have greater medicinal value. Japanese producers of kudzu powder have stated that during World War II, when food was scarce, many Japanese made and ate this partially refined powder, and a large number reported cures of chronic intestinal

ailments. Since the latter product (which is closer to being a whole, natural food) can be produced in less time and at lower cost than its more refined counterpart, it might make sense to produce it in America specifically for medicinal use.

The kudzu plant itself also has several semi-medicinal uses. In Japan ground-up leaves are made into tablets providing supplemental vitamins A and C. Chlorophyll extracted from the leaves is sold in the form of a green powder, mixed with enzymes, and used as a fortifier in a variety of health foods and natural medicines. The white powder is used as a gelatinous base for growing pharmaceutical cultures and as an extender for small amounts of active ingredients requiring capsulization.

In China simple kudzu root decoctions and elaborate kudzu root teas have been used for centuries and perhaps millennia to cure a wide variety of minor and serious ailments. These kudzu preparations are said to be most effective for colds, fevers, influenza, diarrhea, dysentery, and hangovers. John Keys's authoritative *Chinese Herbs* lists kudzu root as a key ingredient in twelve basic medicinal preparations, which are used to treat numerous disorders. Other texts mention that kudzu decoctions are also used to cure snake and insect bites, and to counteract the effects of various poisons; they are externally applied to dog bites. The seeds are used to treat dysentery and relieve hangovers. The flowers, too, are prescribed for hangovers, the leaves are applied to wounds as a styptic. The shoots are simmered in a little milk and applied to incipient boils or cold sores. And every part of the plant is used in the treatment of skin rashes. Kudzu creams are only rarely used.

Kudzu powder and root are also used in traditional herbal medicine in Tibet to cure stomach and intestinal disorders. It is said that the plant (which grows in the Tibetan lowlands) has been highly esteemed since ancient times.

Herbal medicine pouch

Kudzu and Oriental Medicine

The medicinal use of kudzu in Japan dates back more than twelve hundred years. In the *Kojiruien*, a fifty-one-volume encyclopedia compiled between 1896 and 1914, more than twenty-eight pages are devoted to the plant. During the Edo period (1600–1867), when Japanese herbal lore reached the zenith of its sophistication and popularity, kudzu played a key role in the healing process. With the advent of modern chemistry and pharmacology, however, the ancient knowledge was abandoned and kudzu powder came to be better known as an ingredient in fine cuisine.

The first modern figure to take an active interest in kudzu's healing properties was Sagen Ishizuka (1851–1910). In his many public lectures and voluminous writings, he pointed out that kudzu was highly useful in the treatment of a wide variety of ailments. After his death, the nationwide natural-healing movement he began came under the leadership of Manabu Nishihata (1857–1934).

The late Georges Ohsawa (1893–1966), founder of the international macrobiotic movement and the key figure responsible for the revival of kudzu as a medicine in Japan, first learned about the healing root from the writings of Ishizuka and the speeches of Nishihata. As a lad of nineteen, Ohsawa found his physical health rapidly deteriorating, and he ascribed this condition to the fact that his mother had raised him on a Western-style diet including fairly large amounts of dairy products and some meat. When he tried Ishizuka's recommended regimen of whole grains and cooked vegetables, his health improved dramatically. He was soon teaching others about this "new" way of life and eating; like Ishizuka, he advocated the use of kudzu powder as an integral part of the regimen. In his practice Ohsawa used only two kudzu preparations, Kudzu Cream and Kudzu Cream with Salt Plum & Shoyu, for a variety of ailments from colds and diarrhea to dysentery, fever, gonorrhea, headache, and influenza. He eventually brought his teaching to the West, and numbered among his students are Michio Kushi, Noboru Muramoto, and Herman Aihara, who have all been instrumental in popularizing the medicinal use of kudzu in the United States. Mr. Muramoto has perhaps taken the lead through his book, *Healing Ourselves*, and by helping to establish the Herb Tea Company, which distributes Kudzu Root Tea.

Another student of Ohsawa's, Hideo Omori of Shizuoka Prefecture, has continued to develop the medicinal uses of kudzu. Now fifty-seven years old, Omori is known throughout Japan for his remarkable ability to cure diseases by using natural medicines and traditional healing techniques. In his ten years of practice, three thousand people have flocked to his home clinic, and each year thousands more attend his seminars.

Omori first became interested in kudzu in 1961 (before he had ever come in contact with Ohsawa), when he met Kosuké Yamada, a *sennin* (hermit sage) who lived alone in a hut deep in the mountains of Kagoshima Prefecture and devoted himself to Shinto religious practices (including chanting, meditation, breathing exercises, and divination). Struck with the man's vigor, youthful appearance, and lustrous skin, Omori enquired of his age and was astonished to learn that the sage was 102. Having received serious sword wounds as a young man in the Seinan War, Yamada had experienced the transience of the world and decided to lead a life devoted to the realization of Truth. He explained to Omori that his basic foods all grew wild in the mountains. Kudzu powder made into a thick, lightly salted cream was his staple; other foods included wild buckwheat, *jinenjo* (a mountain yam), pinenuts, miscanthus nuts, and wild dog-tooth violet roots (*katakuri*). In later years, Omori met other sennin, including Gingetsu Ito of Yamaguchi Prefecture and Genko Ishi of Kanagawa Prefecture. Though he noted that all these men ate more or less the same diet, he did not perceive the use of kudzu powder as a natural medicine.

Thus, a new perspective opened on his research when he met Georges Ohsawa, twenty-six years his senior, in the early 1960s. The two men quickly became close friends, each sharing his unique perspective and knowledge. Omori learned Ohsawa's two basic medicinal preparations (which he still feels are the most important) and began to study their applicability to various ailments. Impressed with kudzu's effectiveness in the cure of intestinal disorders, diarrhea, and fevers, he gradually expanded his repertoire and its applications by using a variety of healing foods in combination with Kudzu Cream: freshly squeezed apple juice for inducing sweating and knocking out a fever; the juice of (grated) lotus root for asthma, nasal congestion, or a cough; sesame salt for diarrhea; and various *kuroyaki*, or charred substances (especially salt plum and kombu) for a range of more serious diseases. Like Ohsawa, Omori stresses that kudzu powder should generally be used together with a basic diet of brown rice and small amounts of cooked vegetables.

The medical philosophy underlying the movement Ohsawa developed dates back to ancient China and is rooted in the Taoist principle of *yin* and *yang*, or the balance of opposite forces. According to this theory, all foods are viewed as predominantly yin or yang in character (just as Westerners often categorize them as either acidic or alkaline). To be in good health means to be in proper balance. Disease is believed to reflect an imbalance of the yin and yang forces of the body. To cure means to restore the proper balance, and this can be accomplished by eating appropriate foods while refraining from those which first brought about the imbalance.

Kudzu root, like all roots, was traditionally considered very yang in nature and was found to be particularly effective in treating yin disorders. In his work with the root Ohsawa emphasized kudzu's yang qualities. Omori, however, went a step further by pointing out that it is in fact less yang than other curative roots such as ginseng and jinenjo: whereas the latter are both very slender and compact and grow vertically in the soil to great depths (all basic characteristics of yang roots), kudzu roots are often huge and slightly porous and spread in all directions horizontally, and thus are less yang. Moreover, when the root is made into powder, its fibrous portions and skin (both very yang) are removed; the addition of water to make Kudzu Cream adds an additional yin element. Hence, Omori discovered that kudzu could be used even in the treatment of disorders believed to result from an excess of yang force in the body, and particularly those thought to result from an overconsumption of meat, poultry, and eggs. Kudzu heals gently, whereas super-potent ginseng can shock a weakened body, and jinenjo is often hard to digest. In its wide range of applicability, therefore, kudzu is a truly remarkable natural healing agent, capable of curing both yin and yang ailments.

Omori's research among the mountain hermits also led him into another area which Ohsawa had not explored: the idea of using a Thickened or Firm Kudzu Cream instead of grains as the primary food in the diet. Having eaten a rather narrow diet emphasizing lightly salted brown rice or buckwheat for almost fifteen years, Omori decided to experi-

ment with using kudzu powder as his primary food in order to moderate the overly yang constitution he felt he had developed. Thus, for one and a half years he followed a simple regimen consisting of lightly salted, well-thickened Kudzu Cream as his basic food, eaten three times a day, together with miso soup and cooked seasonal vegetables; when semi-fasting, he ate only a very thinned cream. Although his weight dropped slightly (4 pounds), he found that his health was excellent and that he needed less sleep and had more energy than usual. Omori claims that he later succeeded in curing himself of chronic tuberculosis by means of a diet of brown rice and Kudzu Cream. He was so pleased with the results of these experiments that to this day he instructs many of his patients to follow the same menu for breakfast. Omori feels that a similar breakfast diet would be particularly helpful for Americans, with their high consumption of animal products, excessive caloric intake, and high incidence of intestinal and stomach ailments.

While the teachings and writings of healers such as Ohsawa, Omori, Muramoto, Kushi, and Aihara have engendered a growing interest in the medicinal use of kudzu in America, more and more contemporary Japanese are, ironically, opting for modern pharmaceuticals and gradually decreasing their use of kudzu and other ancient healing substances. Among the medicinal kudzu preparations used in Japan today, by far the most popular is Sweetened Kudzu Cream, in which the powder is used together with white sugar. This and other modern preparations will be given later in this chapter, following the unsweetened, basic recipes revived or developed by the teachers mentioned above and now used increasingly in the United States.

MEDICINAL KUDZU ROOT TEAS

Since ancient times in both China and Japan, fresh kudzu roots, gathered from November until April, have been washed, peeled, diced, into 1/8-inch cubes and dried in the sun until they become firm and tan. These cubes, called *kakkon* (a word written with the Chinese characters for "kudzu" and "root"), have long been prized as one of the key ingredients in the traditional art of herbal medicine (*kanpoyaku*). Generally sold in herbal pharmacies, they are packaged—either alone or mixed with other herbs—in small envelopes or sealed jars. A typical dose is 4 to 11 grams. Imported kudzu root has recently begun to appear alongside medicinal herbs such as ginseng, goldenseal, and comfrey on the shelves of herb shops and natural food stores in the United States. We hope that soon kudzu root harvested in the southeastern United States will replace the imported product. The dried cubes could also be sold in prepackaged mixtures such as those described below, or used in creating new varieties of Western-style herbal teas.

Kakkon-to

Kudzu Root Tea (*Kakkon-to*)   MAKES 1½ CUPS

In Japan and China, this mixture of kudzu root and other herbs is one of the most highly esteemed medicinal teas. Sold both in large flow-thru tea bags or as a loose mixture, it has a wonderful fragrance, and a sweet, pungent flavor, somewhat like that of ginseng or *Mu* Tea. Available prepackaged or in bulk from companies in the United States, Japan, and Hong Kong (see appendix A), it can also be found at the wholesale herb stores located in most of America's major Chinese communities (show them the characters reproduced here), or the ingredients can be purchased separately and mixed at home.

In *Healing Ourselves* Muramoto stresses that this tea has many uses. Kudzu Root Tea includes two other basic Oriental medicinal brews: *Mao* and Cinnamon. It is recommended as a specific remedy for chronic headache, stiff shoulders or neck, measles, colitis, upset stomach, breast-feeding difficulties (it stimulates milk flow), sinus troubles, tonsilitis, respiratory ailments (coughing and lung congestion), and even hangovers. Japanese herbalists use it in most of these ways, and in larger doses as a laxative or a diaphoretic (sweat-inducer). The Kudzu Root Tea now sold commercially in the United States contains the following dry ingredients, chopped or ground:

8 grams kudzu root (*Pueraria lobata*)
4 grams ephedra or mao (*Ephedra sinica*)
3 grams cinnamon (*Cinnamomum cassia*)
4 grams unpitted jujube dates (*Zizyphus jujuba*)
1½ grams dried gingerroot (*Zingiber officinale*)
2 to 3 grams licorice (*Glycyrrhiza uralensis*)
3 grams peony root (*Paeonia albiflora*)

To serve: Combine ingredients with 3 cups water in a ceramic or enamel pot. Simmer uncovered for about 45 minutes, or until 1½ cups of liquid remain. Take ½ cup 30 minutes before each meal.

If cold is accompanied by chest pains, anhidrosis, or oliguria, decrease kudzu root to 5 grams and increase dried gingerroot to 4 grams.

Kudzu Root & Magnolia Root Tea (*Kakkon-to Kashinisenkyu*)   MAKES 1½ CUPS

This rather new Japanese preparation, which Masaru Taguchi lists in his book *Oriental Herbal Wisdom*, is used for head colds and general internal problems. To the ingredients for Kudzu Root Tea given above add:

3 grams magnolia root (*Magnolia denudata*)
3 grams cunidium (*Cunidium*)

Prepare and serve like Kudzu Root Tea.

Kudzu Root & Safflower Tea   MAKES 1½ CUPS

This tea is prescribed for those with enlarged hearts—especially if the person has a large red nose (which, according to the Japanese science of physiognomy, is thought to indicate heart trouble).

3 grams kudzu root
3 grams peony root (*Peonia lactifolia*)
3 grams jio root (*Rehmania glutinosa*)
1½ grams safflower
1½ grams gardenia seeds
1½ grams goldthread (*Coptis trifolia*)
1 gram licorice (*Glycyrrhiza uralensis*)

Prepare and serve like Kudzu Root Tea.

MEDICINAL KUDZU CREAMS

The following recipes, each with a slightly different consistency, are used to treat a wide variety of conditions and serve as the basis for several more complex preparations listed according to illness in the following sections. Some of these specific preparations call for the inclusion of charred or carbonized substances (*kuroyaki*, p. 58).

White chunks of kudzu powder, when used directly in their dry form, look and taste remarkably like milk of magnesia and are just as effective in relieving acid indigestion and upset stomach. They need not always be made into a cream to be effective. Undiluted, kudzu can work at full potency to relieve the digestive tract. Simply select a chunk of dried kudzu powder about ½ inch in diameter, place it on your tongue, and allow it to dissolve slowly in your mouth.

Kudzu Cream with Salt Plum & Shoyu (*Ume-sho Kudzu-yu*)

SERVES 1 OR 2

Among the medicinal kudzu-powder preparations, we find this one to be the most effective and versatile. It works particularly well in relieving diarrhea or the aftereffects of overindulging in sweets or of simply overeating; it is also good for acid indigestion, colds, stomach pains, dysentery, and fever. Moreover, it has a delicious flavor and soothing, thick consistency.

Part of the secret of this recipe's effectiveness lies in the use of the salt plum (umeboshi), known in Japan as the king of alkaline foods and as an excellent antidote for acid indigestion or an overly acidic bloodstream. The salt plum is an effective body cleanser, since the picric acid it contains aids the action of the liver and kidneys in removing toxins from the bloodstream. It has been used since ancient times to treat colds, anemia, fatigue, and hangover. Recently, modern Japanese scientists have found that its high-quality citric acid serves to neutralize lactic acid and eliminate it from the body. (Lactic acid is thought to be formed from excess sugar in the bloodstream; it combines with protein and hardens blood vessels, leading to numerous circulatory problems.)

1¼ cups water
1 salt plum (umeboshi), pitted and minced
1½ tablespoons kudzu powder
1 teaspoon natural soy sauce (shoyu)
¼ teaspoon grated or ½ teaspoon powdered gingerroot; or 12 drops juice from grated gingerroot

Combine 1 cup water and the salt plum in a saucepan; bring to a boil. Quickly dissolve the kudzu powder in the remaining ¼ cup water, add to the contents of the saucepan, and, stirring constantly, return to the boil. Reduce heat to low, stir in soy sauce and gingerroot, and simmer for 1 minute. Allow to cool to body temperature. Take one hour before meals, preferably in the morning, when the stomach is empty.

For a thinner consistency, use as little as 1½ teaspoons kudzu powder.

VARIATION

* **Kudzu Cream with Salt Plum, Shoyu & Bancha Tea:** Bancha is a tea made with the three-year-old growth of leaves and twigs picked from the lower branches of the tea bush. To brew: Add 1 to 2 teaspoons dry-roasted bancha twig tea to 2 cups boiling water and simmer for 10 to 20 minutes. Strain well. Substitute for water in the recipe above.

Kudzu Cream (*Kudzu-yu*)

SERVES 1 OR 2

This preparation, which is effective for most of the same ailments as Kudzu Cream with Salt Plum & Shoyu, is so gentle and soothing that it may be used in cases of severe upset stomach when other medicines or foods will not stay down (and when even fasting is not recommended). For minor ailments, the relatively short cooking time recommended here is generally considered sufficient; for more serious ailments or babies' illnesses, Mr. Omori suggests simmering for 10 to 30 minutes (adding a little water as necessary).

1¼ cups water
1½ teaspoons kudzu powder
Dash of natural soy sauce (shoyu) or sea salt

Bring 1 cup water to a boil in a small saucepan. Quickly dissolve kudzu powder in the remaining ¼ cup water, add to the contents of the saucepan and, stirring constantly, return to the boil. Reduce heat to low and simmer for 2 to 3 minutes, or until transparent and well thickened. Stir in soy sauce or sea salt to taste and remove from heat. Serve hot for fevers, but allow to cool to just above body temperature for other ailments.

VARIATIONS

* **With Apple Juice:** See Fever (p. 59).
* **With Grated Lotus Root:** See Cough, Asthma, or Nasal Congestion (p. 59).
* **With Sesame Salt:** See Diarrhea (p. 59).
* **With Charred Substances:** (See p. 58).

Thickened Kudzu Cream (Kudzu-gayu)

SERVES 1 OR 2

Prepare like Kudzu Cream, but increase the amount of kudzu powder to 1½ to 3 tablespoons and simmer for 3 to 5 minutes, or until transparent and nicely thickened.

Firm Kudzu Cream (Kataneri Kudzu-yu)

SERVES 1 OR 2

In Japan, this preparation is considered to be a close relative of mochi. It is served mainly for breakfast (as a substitute for brown rice or other grains), together with miso soup and cooked seasonal vegetables. It is substantial enough to serve as a primary food in the diet.

Prepare like Kudzu Cream, but increase the amount of kudzu powder to 5½ tablespoons and simmer for 5 to 10 minutes, or until very firm.

CHARRED SUBSTANCES IN KUDZU CREAMS

Charred or "carbonized" substances (kuro-yaki) are occasionally used in medicinal Kudzu Creams. In Japan entire books have been written on the healing potency, preparation, and use of such substances. The best-known work, a 246-page tome entitled *Kuroyaki Chiryo Go-hyaku Shu* [five hundred kuroyaki remedies], describes how charred substances have been used since ancient times to treat virtually every type of disease. The most widely used substances are salt plums (umeboshi), kombu, and human hair; other substances include cooked brown rice, salt-pickled eggplant calyxes or caps (the result is sold commercially as Dentie, a natural toothpaste), and even worms and cockroaches. The process for charring transforms most of each substance used into carbon, making it very yang. There are several methods of charring, employing various utensils:

1. *Oven:* This is the easiest method. Place substances to be charred into an uncovered, unglazed earthenware container or on a metal tray. Heat in a 300° to 500°F oven for 25 to 35 minutes, or until well charred and brittle. Allow to cool, then grind to a powder in a mortar or suribachi.

2. *Sealed Pot:* This is the traditional Japanese way. Put substances to be charred into an unglazed earthenware pot and seal lid tightly with *washi* (traditional Japanese paper). Bury in rice husks and ignite the husks; or set on a burner over medium heat for 20 to 30 minutes. Proceed as above.

3. *Foil and Screen:* Wrap substances in aluminum foil and place on a broiling screen over an open flame (or in a hot oven). Proceed as above.

4. *Dry Skillet:* Place substances in a cast-iron skillet and cook, turning occasionally, over medium heat for about 15 minutes, or until charred.

Prepare enough of each substance to have a reserve stock. Suggested quantities: 3 salt plums (good results can be achieved with the oven technique), 1 gram of human hair (preferably charred in a sealed pot), and 30 grams of kombu (good for use with a skillet).

MODERN JAPANESE MEDICINAL PREPARATIONS

Most of the medicinal preparations containing kudzu powder used in Japan today call for sugar. The previous recipes, while quite popular with Japanese and American macrobiotic communities, are not widely known or used by most Japanese. Although we, like many Westerners, prefer to avoid the use of sweetening—particularly white sugar—in medicinal preparations, we wish nevertheless to describe here the most common Japanese preparations.

Three medicinal recipes containing kudzu powder are used in Japan: Sweetened Kudzu Cream (*Kudzu-yu*), which is by far the most popular; Kudzu Cream with Milk (*Kudzu-gayu*), which is described as nutritious and beneficial to those suffering from intestinal ailments; and Milky Chilled Kudzu (*Kudzu-mizu*), which is served both as a hangover remedy and as a refreshing summertime drink. The latter two recipes are given in the section on Kudzu Beverages.

Sweetened Kudzu Cream is prepared by combining 1 teaspoon of kudzu powder, 2 teaspoons of sugar, and 1 tablespoon of water in a small teacup, then mixing well; ½ cup of boiling water is slowly added, and the mixture is stirred constantly, until it becomes transparent. The beverage is then served hot. Alternately, all of the ingredients may be combined in a small saucepan, brought to a boil, and simmered, stirring constantly, for about 1 minute, or until transparent. These proportions of ingredients and methodology are taken from the brochure of one of Japan's most respected manufacturers of kudzu powder. At the end of the recipe, the following words appear: "Provides excellent nutrition for sick people, elderly people, and infants; effective in relieving colds and diarrhea."

In China Kudzu Cream (called *ko-fu* or *ko-rau*) is also usually served sweetened with either sugar or honey. It always contains grated gingerroot and usually a pinch of salt. It is used as a remedy for colds and stomach problems.

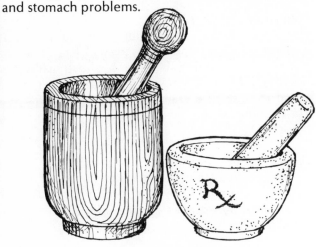

MINOR AILMENTS

With the rapid increase in the cost of institutionalized medicine, the modern reliance on chemical prescriptions, and the danger of inadequately tested, highly toxic products (such as thalidomide), a growing number of people are taking a renewed interest in traditional, natural means of self-healing. Numerous naturopathic healers in both the United States and Japan have found kudzu powder to be effective in the treatment of the following minor ailments. (They also recommend making full use of the body's intrinsic healing capacity by eating only lightly and getting plenty of rest.) We have repeatedly used these preparations ourselves over a period of more than ten years and have found them to be superior to any other medicinal treatments we've tried.

Chills

For a temporary chill, serve a hot cup of plain Kudzu Cream or Kudzu Cream with Salt Plum & Shoyu, until the body is warmed; for a tendency to chill easily, serve daily.

Colds

Serve small portions of Kudzu Root Tea, plain Kudzu Cream, or Kudzu Cream with Salt Plum & Shoyu three times daily. Other than Kudzu Cream, fasting is recommended, to allow energy to be diverted from digestion to cleansing.

Cough, Asthma, or Nasal Congestion

If the patient has a temperature of 100°F or above: Mix 1 part lotus root juice (pressed from freshly grated or puréed root) with 10 parts Kudzu Cream. Take ½ to ¾ cups every hour if the condition is severe; every 3 to 4 hours if less severe.

If the patient's temperature is below 100°F: Bring the lotus root juice (or an equal quantity of freshly grated gingerroot juice) just to a boil before mixing with the Kudzu Cream, then simmer for several minutes with the cream. Use same dosage as above.

Kudzu Cream mixed with Sesame Salt (see "Diarrhea") is also found to be effective.

For general coughing, lung congestion, and other respiratory ailments, Kudzu Root Tea, served in small quantities 30 minutes before light meals, also works well.

Diarrhea

Use Plain Kudzu Cream or Kudzu Cream with Salt Plum & Shoyu. Or use 10 grams of kudzu root to prepare a 1½-cup decoction; take in dosages of ½ cup. Or mix 1 teaspoon sesame salt or ½ teaspoon charred salt plum with ¾ cup Thickened or Firm Kudzu Cream. Take three times daily until condition improves.

(To prepare sesame salt: Combine 3 parts roasted sea salt with 7 parts roasted sesame seeds; grind the mixture to a very fine consistency in a suribachi.)

Fever

Use Kudzu Root Tea, plain Kudzu Cream, or Kudzu Cream with Salt Plum & Shoyu; 1 to 1½ parts apple juice (preferably freshly squeezed from grated or puréed apple) or grated daikon juice may be mixed with 10 parts Kudzu Cream. For fevers accompanying a cold, mix ½ teaspoon charred kombu with ¾ cup Kudzu Cream. Take any of these preparations once each hour until sweating, onced induced, has subsided, and the fever has dropped. Kudzu will alleviate thirst and headache together with the fever. Chinese medicinal texts call for the use of 10 grams of kudzu root to make a 1½-cup decoction; take in dosages of ½ cup three times daily.

Suribachi and wooden p[...]

Hangover

Use Kudzu Root Tea or Kudzu Cream with Salt Plum & Shoyu. Drink ½ to 1 cup in place of the next meal, and repeat every 4 to 5 hours, if necessary. A serving of kudzu noodles also works well. For extreme overconsumption of alcohol leading to alcoholic poisoning, the Chinese recommend the preparation of a decoction made from 4 grams kudzu; a dosage of ½ cup is to be taken only once.

Headache

Use Kudzu Root Tea, plain Kudzu Cream, or Kudzu Cream with Salt Plum & Shoyu. Take in small amounts (½ to 1 cup) at mealtimes in lieu of all other foods.

Indigestion or Dyspepsia

Chinese medicinal texts call for a combination of the following: 5 grams kudzu root, 10 grams *Picrorrhiza kurroa*, 0.5 grams rhubarb (*Rheum officinale*), and 5 grams *Platycodon grandiflorum*. Prepare a 1½-cup decoction and take in dosages of ½ cup.

Inflammations

Use ¾ cup Kudzu Cream (in severe cases add ½ teaspoon charred salt plum) three times daily.

Influenza

Drink ½ to 1 cup Kudzu Root Tea, plain Kudzu Cream, or Kudzu Cream with Salt Plum & Shoyu at mealtimes in lieu of food.

Intestinal and Digestive Disorders

Use plain Kudzu Cream or Kudzu Cream with Salt Plum & Shoyu to provide relief from temporary intestinal disorders, to help restore a weak intestinal tract, or for relief from chronic digestive problems. Take 1 cup each morning in place of breakfast.

Nausea

For nausea accompanied by a gastric fever, Chinese medicinal texts call for the combination of 2 grams kudzu root, 1 gram licorice (*Glycyrrhiza uralensis*), 1 gram unpitted jujube dates (*Zizyphus jujuba*), 10 grams *Phyllostachys puberlua*, and 3 grams *Pinellia tuberifera*. Prepare a 1½-cup decoction and take dosages of ½ cup three times daily.

Overconsumption of Sweets

Use Kudzu Cream with Salt Plum & Shoyu. Take 1 cup instead of the first meal.

Overweight

Use either Thickened or Firm Kudzu Cream in moderate amounts as the main course at mealtimes, together with soup and vegetables. Jelling a cup of liquid with 2 tablespoons of kudzu powder adds only 74 calories while transforming the food from a beverage into the main course of a hearty meal.

Pregnancy and Childbirth

To settle the stomach during the early months of pregnancy, take 1 to 2 cups Plain Kudzu Cream or Kudzu Cream with Salt Plum & Shoyu daily. For puerperal fever, Chinese medicinal texts recommend the use of 8 grams of kudzu root to make a 1½-cup decoction; take dosages of ½ cup three times daily.

Sexual Apathy

Mix 1 to 2 tablespoons grated jinenjo or Tekka Miso (a fermented soybean product available at natural food stores) with ¾ cup Kudzu Cream. Drink 1 to 2 cups daily.

Sinus Congestion

Take small quantities of Kudzu Root Tea 30 minutes before light meals.

Stiffness or Tension

Use Kudzu Root Tea, especially for stiffness of the shoulders or neck; take small quantities 30 minutes before meals.

Stomachache

Generally caused by excess eating or bad food, this condition may often be alleviated immediately by inducing vomiting or, more slowly, by fasting. However, if fasting is too difficult, take small quantities of Kudzu Root Tea, plain Kudzu Cream, or Kudzu Cream with Salt Plum & Shoyu in place of meals. Kudzu works better than fasting to relieve hyperacidity.

Thirst

For extreme thirst accompanying any illness or disease, Chinese medicinal texts call for the use of 8 grams of kudzu root to make a 1½-cup decoction; take in dosages of ½ cup three times daily.

MORE SERIOUS AILMENTS

We list the following applications of kudzu to indicate the extent of its use by traditional Oriental healers. We do not mean to imply that amateurs should use these preparations for self-cure without the guidance of a qualified professional. Most healers who recommend kudzu stress that in the majority of cases, the treatment should be accompanied by a natural food diet consisting primarily of a grain such as brown rice plus small amounts of cooked vegetables.

Anemia

Use Kudzu Grain Coffee in place of other beverages. Or mix Kudzu Cream with several teaspoons of Tekka Miso. Supplement the diet with foods rich in iron (sea vegetables, soybean products, etc.).

Apoplexy

Chinese medicinal texts call for a combination of 7 grams kudzu root, 5 grams *Polygonatum officinale*, 5 grams peony root skin (*Paeonia moutan*), 5 grams garden angelica (*Angelica grosserata*), 3 grams ephedra or mao (*Ephedra sinica*), and 1.5 grams peppermint (*Mentha arvensis*). Chop fine, add 1¾ cups water, and decoct to 1½ cups. Take dosages of ½ cup three times daily.

Bleeding, internal

Mix ½ teaspoon charred salt plum or kombu (or, in serious cases, human hair) with ¾ cup Kudzu Cream. Take three times daily. This treatment is used in cases of bleeding of the intestinal tract, the female reproductive system, or the bladder.

Colitis

Take ½ to 1 cup Kudzu Root Tea, plain Kudzu Cream, or Kudzu Cream with Salt Plum & Shoyu, preferably each morning, several hours before breakfast. As primary foods, serve grains, vegetables, and miso soup.

Dysentery

Use Plain Kudzu Cream or Kudzu Cream with Salt Plum & Shoyu. Take dosages of ½ cup 3 times daily until condition improves. Excellent for chronic dysentery. Or use 10 grams of kudzu root to prepare a 1½-cup decoction and use as prescribed.

Gastroenteritis

Take ½ to 1 cup Kudzu Cream with Salt Plum & Shoyu or ½ teaspoon charred salt plum mixed with ¾ cup Kudzu Cream every 4 to 5 hours.

Gonorrhea

Take 1 cup plain Kudzu Cream or Kudzu Cream with Salt Plum & Shoyu three times daily.

Kidney Ailments

To ¾ cup Kudzu Cream add 2 to 4 tablespoons cooked (whole or mashed) azuki beans or grated jinenjo. Or simmer 1 tablespoon (dry) azuki beans in 2 quarts water until liquid is reduced to 1 quart; season lightly with sea salt and stir in 1 tablespoon kudzu dissolved in 3 tablespoons water. Take 1 cup every 4 to 5 hours.

Measles

For measles accompanied by a fever, Chinese medicinal texts call for the combination of 5 grams kudzu root, 1 gram licorice (*Glycyrrhiza uralensis*), 3 grams peony root (*Paeonia albiflora*), and 8 grams black kohosh (*Cimicifuga foetida*). Prepare a 1½-cup decoction and take dosages of ½ cup three times daily.

Smallpox

Chinese medicinal texts call for the use of 10 grams of kudzu root to make a 1½-cup decoction; take in dosages of ½ cup three times daily.

Tonsilitis or Throat Inflammations

Take ¾ cup Kudzu Cream mixed with 2 tablespoons grated lotus root or ½ teaspoon charred kombu every 4 to 5 hours when temperature is high (over 100°F); if temperature is closer to normal, mix with 2 tablespoons grated apple.

4. Making Kudzu Powder

USING WILD KUDZU and a minimum of equipment, you can prepare fine kudzu powder at home, in a community, or on a commercial scale.

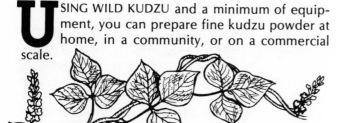

MAKING KUDZU POWDER AT HOME

Tools
A shovel or hoe
A scrub brush
Two 3-to-5-gallon buckets
A knife
A sturdy 2-quart blender, or a food mill or meat grinder
A strainer
A 2-foot-square cotton dishtowel
A 1-gallon wide-mouthed jar
A tray (or paper)

Method
1. Any time between the beginning of December and the end of March, dig up about 5 pounds of kudzu roots. Ideally, each root should be from 1½ to 3 inches in diameter. Using a scrub brush and cold water, wash roots thoroughly in a large bucket. With a sharp, heavy knife, cut off 1½ inches of each root at the stem end and discard. Now cut remaining root crosswise into 1-inch discs.

2. Half-fill a sturdy blender with water. Running it at medium speed, add four to six kudzu discs one at a time and purée until the mixture is quite thick or the blender begins to stall. Pour purée through a strainer set over a bucket. Squeeze the fibrous residue in the strainer to expel as much liquid as possible, then transfer residue to a second bucket. Repeat 6 to 8 times, or until all root sections have been used. (If a blender is not available, cut the root discs into smaller cubes and grind in a food mill or meat grinder. Combine ground root with twice its volume of water, mixing well, then proceed to pour through a strainer as described above.)

3. Add about 1 gallon water to the bucket containing the squeezed fiber. Stir well, then lift out fiber and squeeze by hand over bucket to extract as much liquid as possible; discard fiber. Now pour extracted liquid through the strainer into the first bucket. Squeeze, then discard, any fiber caught in strainer.

4. Stretch a cotton dishtowel over the mouth of the now-empty second bucket and pour in the brown kudzu liquid from the first bucket. Gather ends of cloth, twist closed, and squeeze to express all liquid; discard fibrous residue. Place bucket containing starchy liquid in a cool (preferably cold) place and allow to stand undisturbed for 24 hours while starch settles. Now carefully pour off all the brown liquid that has risen to the surface, and discard.

5. Using a knife, break up claylike starch in bottom of bucket. Refill bucket with cold water, stir until starch is dissolved, then let stand for 24 hours more. Again pour off and discard all liquid that has accumulated.

6. Now break up the kudzu starch and place it in a 1-gallon jar. Rinse out the bucket and pour rinse water into the jar too. Stir starch until it dissolves, then fill jar with cold water and allow to stand for 48 hours in a cool (or cold) place.

7. Pour off water, and carefully scrape off and discard the upper gray layer of impurities until only the pure white clay-like kudzu starch remains. Cut starch into chunks. The kudzu is ready to be used immediately. Or place it on a tray (or several layers of white paper) and set in a cool place to dry for at least 10, preferably 30 to 40 days. When sealed in a container and stored in a cool dry place, the crumbly chunks of well-dried kudzu powder should last indefinitely.

MAKING KUDZU POWDER AS A COMMUNITY

Any group interested in becoming more self-sufficient might find in this traditional, natural process the basis for a cottage industry or small business. Since the work is done primarily during the winter months, it harmonizes nicely with the lull in most farm work. Unprocessed roots could also be diced, dried, and sold as an ingredient for Kudzu Root Tea (see chapter 3).

In old Japan, kudzu powder was often prepared in rural farmhouses and communities quite similar to those now evolving in many post industrial Western countries. The procedure outlined here is derived from the traditional method; communities may wish to introduce some modern adaptations. It is closely related to that for homemade kudzu except that the scale is larger, traditional mallets are used instead of an electric blender or food mill (although these machines may be substituted), and the refining process is more elaborate. We have illustrated the process with a series of old Japanese woodblock prints.

Tools

A hoe (or shovel) and prybar
Backpacks
A mallet and flat stone (or a mortar and pestle)
Two large wooden tubs
A (bamboo) colander
A cloth sack
A wooden rack
A lever or large rock
A wooden pole or paddle
A strainer (cloth or wire)
Several small wooden tubs
A 2-spigoted wooden barrel (or ordinary
　　wooden tub)
Two small wooden buckets
Several trays and paper

Method

1. Any time between the beginning of December and the end of March, dig up mature kudzu roots using a hoe (or shovel) and prybar. Backpack the roots to the processing area.

2. Wash the dirt and sand from the roots, trim stem ends, and cut the roots into 1-to-2-foot lengths. Using a wooden mallet, pound the roots on a flat stone, or grind them in a large mortar with a pestle (or in a mill or grinder) until they are crushed to a pulp.

3. Fill a large wooden tub to three-fourths capacity with clear, cold water (spring or well). Partially immerse a shallow colander in the water and transfer the pulverized roots into it. Now, using both hands, begin to knead and rub the root fibers together in order to wash out the white kudzu starch.

4. Stretch a coarse-weave cloth sack across the mouth of a second large wooden tub. Lift the colander with the well-washed root fibers out of the first tub, drain quickly over that tub, then transfer the fiber into the sack. Pour the starchy liquid from the first tub into the sack (to filter out any fibers), then lift up and drain the sack over the second tub. Slip a wooden rack consisting of 3 or 4 sturdy rods across the tub's mouth, and place the sack on the rack. Twist the sack closed and press the sack with a lever or a heavy rock. (To increase the yield of starch, wash the remaining root fibers again in the first tub, using a small quantity of water, and repeat the filtering and pressing operations.) Discard the root fibers and allow the liquid in the second tub to stand undisturbed in a cold place for 24 hours while the starch settles to the bottom, becoming a solid clay-like layer.

5. Now carefully pour off the liquid supernatant, which contains tannin and other bitter impurities; pour slowly, so that no starch is lost, and discard.

6. Ladle the claylike starch into shallow wooden tubs, mix well with water by stirring with a wooden pole or paddle, and allow to settle for about 5 minutes. Then, using a strainer, skim off any impurities that float to the liquid's surface. Repeat this stirring and skimming process several times, until the water is clear. Then allow the starch to settle for 24 hours. Finally, pour off the liquid, leaving a solid layer of starch.

7. Scoop the starch into a two-spigoted barrel and fill to two-thirds capacity with water. Mix well and allow to stand for 1 hour. Then open the top spigot and drain off the relatively pure starch solution, catching it in a small wooden bucket. Allow this solution to stand for 24 hours, while the starch again settles and solidifies. When the barrel's upper spigot has finished draining, open the lower spigot and drain off the heavier impurities into a second small wooden bucket. Allow these impurities to settle for 24 hours, until solid. (Note: If a two-spigoted barrel is unavailable, use an ordinary wooden tub. Allow the starch to settle until firm, then discard the upper water, and carefully scrape off the upper layer of impurities. Using a knife, scoop out the white kudzu starch and place it in a small bucket; leave the heavy impurities at the bottom of the barrel. Finally, transfer the heavy impurities to a second wooden bucket, and continue to rewash to extract the starch.)

8. Since the starch in the first bucket still contains a small amount of heavy impurities, transfer it back into the spigoted barrel and reprocess it five to seven more times in the same way. And since the heavy impurities in the second bucket still contain some of the precious kudzu starch, rewash them in the spigoted barrel three more times. With each washing, collect the freshly processed starch in the starch bucket and collect the heavy impurities in a separate bucket.

9. When the kudzu starch has reached the desired degree of whiteness and mildness of flavor (ascertained by tasting), scrape it out of the bottom of the bucket, break it into pieces about the size of a person's hand, and spread it on paper-lined wooden trays (preferably slatted for air circulation) arranged in the shade. Dry for at least 10 (preferably 30 to 40) days, until crumbly.

MAKING KUDZU POWDER IN A COMMERCIAL SHOP

All the kudzu powder sold today in the West is imported from Japan, and virtually all of this is made in one of that country's five major shops (see appendix A). We feel that America is ready to support at least several domestic kudzu processors, who could provide us with a quality product made from domestically grown kudzu at prices far below the present import price.

Processing—a simple, natural operation, by and large—fits in with the ecology of kudzu's preferred habitat. There are only three requirements for locating a shop to prepare fine kudzu powder.

1. *It must be near an abundant supply of pure, cold water.* The more water used in the refining process, the higher the quality of the final product. The water must be cold to avoid fermentation. Only pure water will give pure-white kudzu powder with the finest flavor. The Japanese have always attached great importance to the quality of the water used in preparing traditional foods such as sake, natural soy sauce (shoyu), tofu, miso, and kudzu powder. Several centuries ago it was not uncommon for wealthy tea lovers in Tokyo to dispatch special messengers in palanquins to fetch the very finest mountain water from Kyoto, over three hundred miles away. The site of Japan's oldest shop making kudzu powder (still in the same family after four centuries) is said to have been chosen primarily for its plentiful supply of clear mountain water; Japan's largest shop, Hiro Hachido, now uses 1,320 tons of water a day!

2. *The weather during the winter must be fairly cold and clear.* The air, as well as the water, must be cold, or the abundant natural sugars in the kudzu starch, activated by minute amounts of bacterial enzymes, will begin to ferment, imparting a slightly "off" flavor. (For this reason, the kudzu powder produced in semitropical areas such as Taiwan is considered somewhat inferior.) Those interested in producing high-quality kudzu powder in the United States might want to do their processing in a relatively cold climate and import unprocessed roots or semiprocessed starch from the warmer southeastern states. Yoshino, where the climate is considered ideal, has an average yearly temperature of 56°F and average rainfall of 71 inches. The soil is soft and fertile. At 34° North Latitude it is located in a valley 1,000 feet above sea level, surrounded by mountains 2,000 to 2,500 feet tall.

3. *Plenty of high-quality roots containing a large percentage of starch must grow nearby.* Good roots generally grow in nutrient-rich (or well-fertilized) soil in a dry climate with plenty of sunlight. Larger diameter roots are usually richest in starch. (Small roots found growing in poor soil in a shady exposure or wet climate may contain very little starch.) Roots suitable for processing contain, on the average, 20 to 28 percent starch; it is concentrated at the root's center and least abundant near the surface. Roots containing less than 10 percent starch are not worth processing. It is said that the best-quality roots will sink when placed in water; those which float are inferior. All roots should be processed fresh, since the amount of starch decreases the longer the root is stored.

The production of kudzu powder follows a yearly cycle which perfectly complements the standard agricultural schedule. The season for gathering roots begins in early December, when the plant has finished its yearly growth and the starch is drawn down into the roots, where it remains during the cold winter months—mixed, however, with bitter tannin, which must be removed during the refining process. (In southern Japan, the kudzu plant is often called *kanné*, which literally meals "cold root.") The season lasts only until the beginning of April, when the first spring greenery begins to appear on the vines. At this time, the starch is drawn up out of the roots to provide energy for the new growth. (Roots gathered any later contain such a low yield of starch that it is not worthwhile to process them; furthermore, as the water and air begin to warm, processing becomes unfeasible.) When rice planting begins in mid-April, workers employed by companies making kudzu powder are again free for farm work. In September, as the farming season comes to an end and the air and water begin to cool, they return to the kudzu shops to further refine the previous season's substandard starch. This work is usually completed by the time kudzu harvesting resumes in December.

The process for extracting kudzu powder from the plant's roots is said to have been developed during the 1200s in Shimane Prefecture, whence it gradually spread to the other provinces. The first shop to produce kudzu powder commercially in Japan was started in 1616 by Yuemon Morino, a former attendant to the emperor. Located in the small village of Shimo-ichi near Nara Prefecture's Mount Yoshino, Morino's shop was the start of the present-day Yoshino Morino Kudzu Company. It was the kudzu powder from this shop, and later from other shops in the vicinity, that gradually became known throughout Japan as "Yoshino Kudzu." From 1716 to 1736, the process was expanded and refined by the famous Tosuke Morino, and in 1818 the basic method was taken from Yoshino to Japan's main southern island of Kyushu by Hirota Kyusuké, who started the Hirokyu shop in Fukuoka Prefecture's Akizuki. In 1828 the noted agriculturist Nagatsuné Okura wrote *Sei-kudzu Roku*, the first detailed description of the method for kudzu powder production. By the beginning of the Meiji period (1867) small kudzu shops were in operation throughout Japan. A new center of production had developed near Hodatsu Mountain in Ishikawa Prefecture, where eighty shops prospered. Records show that Nara Prefecture (including the Yoshino area) had twelve shops, a number of which were famous throughout Japan. Following World War II, with the development of Western methods for processing potato and corn starches, the number of shops decreased rapidly, until by 1960 only twenty were left.

The areas most famous for kudzu powder were Yoshino in Nara Prefecture, Akizuki in Fukuoka Prefecture, Kumakawa in Kyoto Prefecture, Hodatsu in Ishikawa Prefecture, Katsuyama in Okayama Prefecture, and Honyama in Hyogo Prefecture. At present, almost all production of kudzu powder in Japan is concentrated around two areas: Nara Prefecture, south of Kyoto; and Kagoshima, a scenic port town surrounded by mountains, located at the southern tip of Japan's southernmost main island, Kyushu. Although Nara has traditionally been the center for all phases of kudzu powder production, little harvesting is being done there now; today most starch comes from roots gathered in the mountains of Kyushu. There are three reasons for this trend: (1) Nara's winters are considerably harsher, and the few people still willing to do such rigorous outdoor work in so cold a climate expect much higher wages than are customary in Kyushu; (2) after centuries of intense harvesting, Nara no longer presents an abundance of readily accessible mature plants; (3) kudzu roots from Kyushu are found to yield more starch than those from Nara, since much of the latter's growing area is now shaded by dense stands of cedars. As a result, the companies making kudzu powder in Nara Prefecture prefer to refine semiprocessed kudzu starch (which looks like a beige clay) bought from Kyushu companies, rather than harvest native roots. Today, Japan's largest producer of refined kudzu starch, Hiro Hachido, is located near Kagoshima and the company employs about 150 men just to bring in roots from the nearby mountains.

There are about nine major shops making kudzu powder in Japan today (the five largest are described in appendix A), plus an unknown number of small shops scattered in remote mountain villages. The shops in the Nara area have, for the most part, retained the traditional techniques and tools: for example, they still tend to use hand-processing methods and wooden tubs in preference to machinery and large concrete tanks. Even the more modernized shops approach their task with a sense of reverence for tradition; they are concerned about the purity of their all-natural ingredients (wild kudzu roots and clear stream water) and take pride in the quality of their finished product. Since about 80 percent of their kudzu powder is sold to fine Japanese confectionery shops and much of the remainder to natural food companies, there is a strong demand to keep standards high.

The Japanese (who prize white rice, white sugar, and white bread) attach great importance to producing pure white kudzu powder. The 60 to 90 days required to create such a product inevitably raises the price. By abbreviating some of the many repeated rewashings in the Japanese process, American makers could lower their production costs, while simultaneously obtaining a greater yield of the final powder having a greater jell strength. (As explained in chapter 3, this off-white kudzu powder is thought to have greater medicinal value than its popular, more highly refined counterpart.)

The commercial method of preparing kudzu powder has not changed substantially in four hundred years. The only real difference is that today, a number of machines (saws, pulverizers, pumps, vibrators, centrifuges, and mixers) have been introduced to make the process easier, more efficient, and less costly.

The following illustrated sequence, drawn from the procedure followed at the Hiro Hachido shop, Japan's principal exporter of kudzu powder, typifies the commercial process:

In early December the wild kudzu roots are dug from the mountains; oxen are sometimes used to help pull up large roots. (Roots have been found measuring over 12 inches in diameter and 7 feet in length, and weighing as much as 440 pounds.) Care is taken in harvesting not to cut the roots, lest fermentation begin, which lowers the quality of the final kudzu powder.

The roots are cut into 3-foot lengths with a handsaw. Now resembling a stack of dirt-encrusted firewood, the roots are tied onto backpacks, and carried out to the nearest road.

The firm, fibrous roots are scraped to remove any caked dirt or stones which might damage the saw blades. Typical roots average 2 to 3 inches in diameter; very small roots are rejected. The woody upper portions of the roots are trimmed off and discarded.

The roots are then washed and cut crosswise with an electric rotary saw into 1½-inch-thick discs.

There they are loaded onto a large truck, which transports them to the processing shop.

The discs drop into a box below the saw, where they are pulverized by a rapidly spinning roller covered with tiny teeth; cold mountain water is pumped in with the fibrous mash to form a slurry, or watery mixture.

The crude fiber is filtered out by pumping the slurry over a series of shallow, vibrating 3-by-6-foot trays mounted at an angle of 30 degrees and lined with a 40-mesh (40 holes per linear inch) silk screen.

The milky grayish solution, which contains the kudzu starch, filters through the screen and is then pumped onto a similar 100-mesh screen tray. The root fibers slide off the end of the 40-mesh tray and are again mixed with cold water, and the mixture is filtered through four more 40-mesh screen trays. After each filtering, the starch washed out of the fibers is pumped over to the 100-mesh tray. After the final washing and filtering, the clean fiber is removed by a

conveyor belt and stored for future sale as fodder, fertilizer, or a hemp substitute. Any fiber particles that accumulate atop the 100-mesh screen are also vibrated off and mixed with water; they are finally pumped onto the last of the 40-mesh screens, filtered once more, and removed for storage.

The starchy solution that has passed through the 100-mesh screen is then pumped onto a slanted, nonvibrating 300-mesh screen and washed from above with a gentle, fine spray of water. (Any fibers remaining on this screen are again mixed with water, filtered through the last of the 40-mesh screens, and stored.)

The solution that has passed through the 300-mesh screen, now completely free of cellulose fiber and other coarse particles, is pumped into a centrifuge, where it is condensed to one third of its original volume. (The clear water constituting the remaining two thirds is discarded.) The concentrated, muddy, grayish-brown solution (its relative density is 1.05; i.e., it is 5% heavier than water) is pumped into a 15-foot-diameter, 3-foot-deep concrete tank and

allowed to settle for 30 minutes. Protein, ash, tannin, mud, and other impurities sink to the bottom, while the white starch remains dissolved and suspended in the water. This starch solution is now carefully pumped off into a 10-foot-square, 3-foot-deep concrete tank and allowed to settle for 48 hours.

The impurities remaining on the bottom of the round tank are mixed three times with fresh water and allowed to settle each time in order to remove all the usable starch; the impurities are then discarded.

After 48 hours, a 1-inch-thick layer of claylike grayish starch settles to the bottom of the square tank. Most of the 3 feet of water above this starch is pumped off and discarded. (The last ¼ inch of water just above the firm layer of starch is carefully pumped back into the round tank and mixed with the next batch of starch solution in order to avoid wasting any of the precious kudzu starch.) The firm starch residue remaining on the bottom of the square tank is shoveled into drum cans and moved elsewhere for further processing. Generally, 100 pounds of kudzu roots yield 15 to 20 pounds of this semiprocessed starch, known in Japan as *sosei kudzu*.

Placed now in one of many 8-foot diameter, 3-foot-deep concrete tanks, the solid starch is mixed with clear water to form a thick solution with a relative density of 1.16. This solution is stirred for several minutes with a large motor-driven rotating paddle, then allowed to settle for 5 minutes.

The kudzu starch sinks to the bottom of the tank, and this time, because of the higher density of the solution, the small proportion of tannin and other remaining light impurities float to the surface where they mix with a layer of bubbles; a large

screen skimmer is used to remove them. This process of stirring, allowing the starch to settle for 5 minutes, and then skimming off the scumlike impurities is repeated about 40 times in the round tank.

The starch-and-water solution is then pumped into an adjacent 7-foot-square, 3-foot-deep tank and allowed to settle for 48 hours. When the starch has settled to the bottom, the water is discarded; then fresh water is mixed with the starch in the square tank and the mixture is pumped back into the round tank. This entire cycle of stirring and settling (40 times in the round tank for 5 minutes each, then 48 hours in the square tank) is repeated a total of 5 or 6 times and takes about 16 days. Gradually all of the gray color and bitter tannin are removed, leaving only pure-white, mild-tasting kudzu starch.

In the final repetition of the cycle, the starch is allowed to settle for 48 hours in the round tank, and a 2-inch-thick, solid layer of kudzu starch forms on the bottom. The top and bottom surfaces of this layer, which contain minute amounts of impurities, are carefully scraped off and set aside for additional refinement. The surface scrapings from five such batches are mixed together with fresh water in a separate square tank and allowed to settle for 48 more hours. Eventually, the slightly lower quality starch which has been removed from the upper and

Then the clear water above the pure kudzu starch is pumped off, and the remaining 6-inch-thick layer of pure white, claylike starch is cut into large blocks with a flat-bladed spade.

lower surfaces of the pure kudzu starch is collected, further refined, and dried, then sold as one type of second-grade *nami-kudzu* (see appendix B).

The pure central portion of the kudzu starch is mixed with the other pure starch, and the mixture is dissolved in fresh water. This solution is filtered through a 300-mesh screen into a 3-foot-deep 6-by-3-foot cement tank lined with a clean white cloth; here it is allowed to settle for 15 hours.

These blocks are placed in a cloth-lined wheelbarrow and transferred to the drying room, where they are cut with a small knife or broken by hand into pieces about 3 inches square and 1 inch thick. These small slabs are placed into a large number of 4-inch-deep wooden boxes, each measuring about 18 by 24 inches. The bottoms of these boxes consist of $1/8$-inch-diameter reeds, which allow air to circulate; each box is lined with a layer of white paper or newsprint.

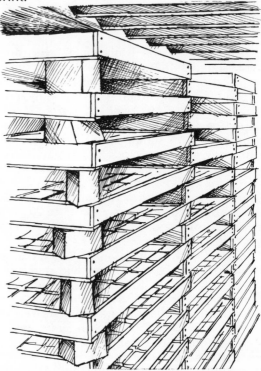

Drying takes place indoors in the shade, at the natural temperature of the region. The average time needed for thorough drying is 45 days; in very cold or wet weather as much as 90 days may be required, whereas in hot, dry weather as little as 20 days may be sufficient. Kudzu starch that dries slowly, during the early, colder part of the kudzu-harvesting season, tends to form hard lumps; starch that dries more quickly, in the later, warmer months, tends to be softer and more crumbly. This difference in texture, however, does not affect flavor and jell strength of the final product.

When dried, each cake of dried kudzu starch now contains only 16.5 percent moisture. The upper surface is carefully cleaned with a soft hair brush to remove any dust that may have accumulated while the kudzu was drying, then crumbled to form the chunky kudzu powder.

Kudzu powder for wholesale is weighed into 11-pound (5-kilo) quantities, sealed in plastic bags, and packaged in wooden boxes. For retail in Japan or the West, it is packaged in 4-ounce cellophane bags.

5. Weaving with Kudzu

KUDZU VINES yield strands of high-quality bast fiber that have been used for over 750 years by folk artisans and commercial weavers throughout East Asia to produce fine textiles. Extracted by hand, the fibers are prized above all for their translucent, almost radiant luster (generally considered to be even finer than that of silk), their attractive ivory-to-beige color, which seems to be burnished with a tint of gold, and their strength. In both texture and appearance, they somewhat resemble the clear flax used to make fine linen. The filaments used for weaving are made by splitting the fibers lengthwise; each is markedly flat and as thin as paper. Most modern artisans use the filaments in their natural form (without spinning, twisting, or dyeing), to allow the inherent beauty of the basic material itself to shine through. Kudzu cloth is always woven on hand looms, since its irregular fibers take poorly to mechanical treatment.

There are four basic types of kudzu cloth. The one most popular in America is kudzu grasscloth, an elegant wallpaper that adds its warm and natural beauty to the interior decor of many thousands of homes; few people realize that this product, generally sold simply as "grasscloth," is made from kudzu. Two varieties of very thin cloth (one tight and one loose weave) are used both for garments and for nonutilitarian decorations; ideal for summer wear, they are not as soft and pliant as silk, yet more delicate than coarse linens or hemp cloth. A final type is used to make netting.

A BRIEF HISTORY OF KUDZU CLOTH

Studies by Japanese anthropologists and historians indicate that kudzu was first used for weaving by Mongols living in the mountains north of the great wall of China; they used (and still use) whole vines to fashion baskets, pack trumplines, and suspension bridges. Gradually the craft was transmitted southward to China, where documents dating from the third century A.D. mention that fibers extracted from kudzu vines were used to make lightweight summertime garments; some were presented as an offering to the emperor.

Scholars believe that in Japan, split kudzu vines were fashioned into coarsely woven goods such as fences or baskets, and even woven into primitive clothing as early as the Jomon period, just prior to the Christian Era. By the end of the Yayoi period (A.D. 200), weaving techniques had apparently become quite refined. The origin of kudzu cloth in Japan is usually traced to a legend. One day an old woman living in the village of Amagata, 10 miles northwest of the town of Kakegawa in Shizuoka Prefecture, noticed that a vine growing next to a waterfall had been flayed by the water until its outer skin had been worn away, leaving only a number of lustrous white filaments. Cutting a number of similar vines, which she recognized as kudzu, she extracted the fibers, washing them repeatedly in water, and wove them into a cloth that she presented to the feudal lord of Kakegawa. The lord named the waterfall *Kappu-no-taki* ("Kudzu-Cloth Falls") and encouraged his subjects to begin producing the cloth and to make it famous throughout Japan.

A later legend, now often reported as historical fact, has it that Kobo Daishi, a great Japanese Buddhist saint born during the eighth century, wore robes made of kudzu cloth while practicing meditation in the mountains near Mount Yoshino.

During the Heian period (794—1185) it was customary for the bodies of the dead to be clothed in white. Archaeological studies have shown that a finely woven cloth made from sun-and-water-bleached kudzu cloth was widely used for this purpose.

The first written reference to the cloth's use in Japan appeared during the Kamakura period (1185–1382), when it was said that a lord from the town of Kakegawa offered kudzu cloth at the Hachi-mangu Tsurugaoka Shrine in the capital at Kamakura. Used to a limited extent during this period to make hunting garments and funeral robes, it first came to be well known throughout Japan during the Edo period (1600–1867). Kakegawa, now the center of kudzu cloth production, was one of the fifty-three stations on the well-traveled Tokaido Road joining Tokyo and Kyoto. A book written in the 1660s describes how there were as many looms in the town as there were inns, and how their busy sound filled the air. The weavers made *hakama* (men's split skirts) for the many horseback riders, *kamishimo* (ceremonial upper garments), *jinbei* (three-quarter-length coats), and summertime *juban* (long undergarments). Much of this clothing was made from 1-foot-wide indigo-dyed cloth woven into attractive patterns. From about 1690, the weavers began to make *noren* (curtains hung at the entranceways to restaurants), summertime coverings for *zaboton* (cushions), and *yagu* (bedclothes). The great artist Hokusai made a woodblock print of Kakegawa women selling bolts of kudzu cloth.

Selling kudzu cloth, seventeenth century

Since earliest times, folk weavers throughout the Japanese provinces had made a cloth generally called *fuji-nuno*, which was woven from the natural fibers of either wild mountain wisteria (*fuji*) or wild kudzu; the two plants were considered to be so similar in use and appearance that the latter was usually called *kudzu fuji* rather than simply kudzu.

Coarsely woven material, prized for its durability, resistance to tearing, and relative impermeability to wind and rain, was used mostly for work clothes, especially jackets, but in some cases pants or hakama. Fine white cloth was used for funeral garments, partially because of its lovely white color and partially because of its name: the word *fuji* means "do not die" and has the connotation of eternal life. The production of the cloth, woven in farmhouses for personal use, apparently reached its peak at the end of the Meiji period in about 1912. Yet by 1935, when the scholar of Japanese folk crafts and customs, Tsuneichi Miyamoto, began his lengthy travels in the provinces, he found kudzu cloth being produced almost everywhere he went. And the tradition remains very much alive in some provinces to this day.

Starting in 1868, with the Meiji reformation and its Westernization of Japan, commercial demand for traditional clothing made from Kakegawa-style kudzu cloth began to decrease. Soon, however, looms were developed to produce a high-quality, 3-foot-wide kudzu grasscloth that was used initially as a covering on *fusuma* (sliding doors); by 1887 it had begun to be exported to the United States, where it became popular as a fashionable yet simple and natural wallpaper. To supply the rapidly growing demand for kudzu grasscloth, Japan began to import large quantities of kudzu fiber from Korea, where the plants were already being cultivated. Kakegawa continued to be the center of production, reaching its heyday in about 1955, when forty households using four hundred looms turned out 130,000 tons of woven goods. In 1962, however, the industry underwent a sudden change: Korea decided to stop exporting kudzu fiber and use it instead to weave Korean goods for export. Within a decade the center of kudzu cloth production had shifted to Korea, where the industry surpassed Japan's record outputs and became foremost supplier to the world. Japan's failure to cultivate kudzu, combined with the country's rising wage scale, made a comeback impossible; by 1977 Kakegawa had only three households and ten looms at work.

Since early times, another center of kudzu cloth production in Japan was the city of Karatsu in Saga Prefecture, where a netlike fabric was woven from a twine of twisted kudzu filaments. Because of competition from synthetic fibers such as nylon, this industry died out in 1975.

Reports from China state that the ancient craft of weaving kudzu cloth is still being practiced; the most famous area of production is located near the headwaters of the Yangtze River.

MAKING KUDZU FIBER FILAMENTS

In Japan the filaments made by tying together lengths of split kudzu fiber are called *kudzu-o* (literally, "kudzu flax"). Requiring almost no initial investment, this craft makes an excellent seasonal job. The work of extracting and drying the fibers, then coiling them into hanks, is generally done during the summer. In the fall, the individual lengths are tied end to end, wound on bobbins, and in some cases dyed. Winter and spring are the seasons for weaving.

At the peak of the harvesting season a worker can gather as much as 245 pounds of fresh kudzu vines per day. However, it takes about 52 pounds of vines to make 1 pound of finished filaments. The process takes 3 to 6 days and requires such constant attention that a Japanese proverb says: "Those who make kudzu-o are too busy even to visit their best friend's deathbed."

The method described here is that used to supply the looms at Kakegawa. The work is done primarily by about twenty women (most of them in their sixties), working with kudzu that grows at the headwaters of the Kakegawa River near the famous waterfall. A 25-minute color film made in 1975 (see appendix B) depicts the process.

Kudzu vines are gathered fairly young, when they are green and pliant, generally from early June until late July (plants harvested in late summer have stiff fibers). Only straight first-year vines (growing directly out of the crown) are used; these lie right on the ground and are free of tangles. Vines growing down a river bank and into the water are ideal. The best vines are fat and at least 6 (preferably 12 to 15) feet long with leaves set well apart. Each vine is cut off near its base with a sickle; then the leaves are stripped off by running the hand down the vine, from base to tip. When twenty to thirty vines have been cut, their base ends are gathered and tied with a short length of vine; then they are wound into a coil 18 to 24 inches in diameter and secured in several places with rope or twine. The coils are placed in the shade or immersed in water.

The ideal work place is one located on a bank above a clean stream. A 2-to-3-foot-diameter caldron or open-ended drumcan with a door at the base of one side is placed over a fire pit. The caldron is three-quarters filled with water and brought to a boil over a hot fire. One or two coils are immersed in the water, which is returned to the boil over high heat, and the coils are cooked covered, for 20 to 25 minutes, or until the outer layer of skin has turned brown and begins to separate from the stalk as the former becomes saturated with boiling water. (When shallow pots are used, they are filled halfway, and covered with a lid; each side of the coil is steamed for 30 minutes.) The coils are taken immediately to the nearby stream and immersed in slowly circulating water, in an area having a sandy or pebbly (not muddy) bottom. They are secured with a stone and allowed to soak for 24 hours, while some of the outer bark is removed by the gentle action of the current. The remaining coils are boiled and immersed in the same way.

Meanwhile a fermenter is prepared on a gradually sloping hillside above the river. A hole is dug, about 1 foot deep and large enough to contain the coils (3 to 6 feet wide and 6 to 9 feet long). If the ground is muddy, the bottom of the hole is lined with sand or pebbles, then topped with a 4-inch-thick layer of straw followed by a 3-inch-thick layer of green grass; the Japanese prefer *susuki* (Japanese pampas grass, or *Mascanthus sinensis*) and/or *kaya* (*Torreya nucifera*). The coils are removed from the river and drained for several minutes, then stacked in the fermenter so that each coil partially overlaps the one below it.

They are covered with three inches of green grass followed by 4 inches of straw; then the entire hole is covered with one or two sheets of reed or rice-straw matting secured in six to eight places with rocks and allowed to stand for 48 hours. After 24 hours, the covering is lifted, to check that the temperature is slightly warmer than body temperature. If it is above 104°F, some of the covering is removed; if below 95°F, more covering and rocks are added. At the end of 48 hours the surface of several coils is examined. Each kudzu vine is composed of two concentric layers of fiber that cover a long core of woody tissue. The outer skin and inner core must be removed in order to make use of the pliant layer of long fibers between them. Fermentation brings about a slight decomposition of the outer skin, causing it to become somewhat mushy; when rubbed, it separates easily from the layer below it and comes off.

The coils are returned to the river shallows, immersed in the circulating water, secured with a stone, and allowed to soak for about one hour, or until much of the outer layer of skin has come off. The coil is then untied with one hand, held underwater at the base, so that the loose tip ends float downstream. Starting at the base end, one or two vines at a time are grasped between thumb and forefinger, and the remaining outer layer of skin is stripped off and pulled down toward the loose ends. The base end is rolled up to form a coil.

When the first washing is completed, the coils are taken to a dry, shady area. All the vines from one coil are placed in a straight line across the lap, with their base ends to the right and tips to the left. The artisan grasps the base end of one vine with the thumb and forefinger of the right hand, then used the small fingers of the left hand to very carefully work the second concentric sheath of kudzu fibers down toward the tip of the vine (as if pulling the skin off a snake), while the woody core is simultaneously being pulled out with the right hand. When the cores of all the vines have been pulled out, about thirty of the second sheaths are stretched out (before being stretched they looked like large wrinkled caterpillars) and their base ends are gathered, together. The same process is repeated for the remaining second sheaths.

The bundles of fibrous sheaths are taken to the river and, held in the current as previously, given a second washing. The fingers are used very gently to comb the fibers along their full length, while separating them into ever finer strands and washing out all of the vine's remaining natural starch. After about an hour of such washing, the supple white filaments wave in the current like a long silken banner. They are then wound onto the extended thumb and little finger in the form of a figure eight. (An optional soaking in rice-bran water will give a slightly whiter color and softer texture. A 20-gallon tub is filled with water to two thirds; then 1 gallon of rice bran is placed into a cloth sack and kneaded for several minutes underwater, until the water turns milky. The sack is removed; the kudzu fiber is dropped in and allowed to soak for 6 hours, then rinsed well in clear water.)

The base ends of the strands (which should average 9 to 12 feet in length) are gathered, looped into loose hanks, and wrung firmly by hand to expel excess water. They are then draped over a clothesline or pole to dry and bleach in the sun for 3 to 6 hours. The hanks are shaken three or four times during this period to aid drying and prevent tangling. Then the hanks are unwrapped, given a final shaking, rewrapped carefully in neat hanks, and placed near a 2½-foot-diameter shallow wooden tub.

A single kudzu filament is pulled from the first hank, and, starting from the base end, using the fingertips, split into several narrower strips, which

are combed out to the tip. The strips' width depends on the type of cloth for which they are to be used (see "Weaving Kudzu Cloth"): for very fine splitting, a needle point is used. The split fibers (whose length should average 3 feet or more) are placed in the tub. When all of the fibers have been split, two are selected and tied head to tail, using any compact knot; the knot is rolled firmly between

thumb and forefinger to compress it. In quick succession all the kudzu fibers are tied head to tail to form a single, long filament, which is coiled simultaneously to a length of about 250 feet.

With a chopstick held in the left hand, the filament is wound onto the stick in a figure-eight form to make a bobbin. When it is full, the stick is pulled out, leaving a bobbin 6 inches long weighing about 11 grams (3/8 ounce). In Japan, such bobbins sold for about $4.80 each in 1977; a typical artisan could tie and wrap about nine per day.

WEAVING KUDZU CLOTH

In Japan, Korea, and China, kudzu filaments have been used to make at least four different types of cloth, the more tightly woven of which are quite water-resistant. In Japan, the first three (all called *kappu*) were produced primarily in Kakegawa; the fourth (called *kudzu-fu*) was made only in the city of Karatsu in Saga Prefecture. The first type is most popular in China; the third, in Korea. Samples of all four types (including samples produced 250 years ago) can be seen at Kawade Shoten in Kakegawa (see appendix A). As kudzu cloth woven by folk artisans has become more of a rarity in Japan, it has grown in esteem and increasingly can be seen at folk museums throughout the country. The cloth's remarkable durability has given rise to a proverb that says that the first generation wears it as a jacket, the second generation as a shirt, and the third as an undergarment. A little stiff at the beginning, it softens and mellows nicely with age.

Kudzu is generally used as the weft (cross-threads), together with a warp of fine cotton or linen thread. Shortly before use, each bobbin is rolled in about 2 tablespoons of water in order to just moisten all the fibers, thereby keeping them soft and pliant. If used as the warp, the hanks (before being wound onto bobbins) should be dipped into a light paste solution of whole wheat or buckwheat flour and water, wound around two vertical posts placed about 10 feet apart, such that no two adjacent lengths of the filament touch one another, and allowed to dry. The light paste coats the filament just enough to prevent it from shredding as it passes through the heddle.

1. **Kimono Cloth (narrow fiber, tight weave):** This rather thin, lightweight cloth has a soft, pliant, almost papery texture resembling that of the modern (often disposable) textiles made from soft paper. Generally used to make clothing, it was traditionally fashioned into hakama and kamishimo, etc.; today it is woven only rarely. (It is still made, however, by the weaver Tsugio Odani of Arashiyama near Kyoto, who is famous for his indigo kudzu-cloth kimonos.) In most cases the cloth is made from dyed kudzu filaments; the entire bobbin is immersed in the dye-stuff, thereby producing subtly different shades along the threads. Because of their unique translucence, the filaments take the dye beautifully and attain an unusual degree of natural luster. Japan's great master of traditional dyeing, 80-year-old Shoichi Goto of Osaka, has produced many lovely creations using kudzu cloth. His favorite dye—and the traditional favorite—is indigo, but folk weavers also use safflower, mountain peach, and others.

Directions:

Using a needle point, split the fibers into very slender filaments; tie into long strands, wind on bobbins, and dye if desired. Thread a hand loom with a warp of 40 to 60 slender cotton, linen, or silk threads per inch. Place the dyed bobbin into a shuttle and weave the cloth tightly. Remove the cloth from the loom and trim off any protruding ends. To make the cloth softer, more pliant, and more lustrous, it is usually fulled (pounded). Wrap it at least ten times around a 12-inch-wide board, slide out the board, and place the folded cloth on a firm wooden fulling block. Using a 5-inch-diameter, 4-

inch-long wooden mallet, pound the cloth firmly, two or three times in each spot, over its entire surface. Turn the cloth over and repeat. For extra softness, knead it gently. (Both processes break the filaments into minute consecutive joints.) To give the cloth added durability, make a paste using kudzu powder and water, and paint this on one side of the cloth as a backing. To make the cloth water-repellent, paint it with the tart liquid extracted by simmering bitter persimmons in water.

2. **Summer Cloth (narrow fiber, fairly loose weave):** This lightweight, partially transparent fabric is slightly coarser than that described above. Resembling a light hemp cloth or coarse linen, it was traditionally dyed and used to make summertime clothing such as *jinbei* (three-quarter-length coats); today it is used largely undyed to make scroll backings, handbag coverings, placemats, summer floor cushion covers (that are cool to sit on), door curtains and room dividers (which blow in the breeze and create the feeling that it is much cooler than it actually is), and *obi* (wide, decorative belt sashes for the kimono).

Directions:
Split the fibers almost as fine as those above. Use a warp of 24 slender cotton threads and weave fairly loosely. Full lightly.

3. **Grasscloth (wide fiber, loose weave):** This is the fabric used for the popular kudzu grasscloth wallpaper that presently accounts for 80 to 90 percent of the total kudzu cloth production in Korea and Japan. The 3-foot-wide grasscloth comes in a 24-foot-long roll which in 1977 sold for $66 wholesale.
Directions:
Using your fingertips, split the fibers into widths of about 1/16 inch. Use a warp of 12 thin but strong cotton threads per inch. Weave quite loosely. After trimming, press in a large screw press instead of fulling, then attach a backing of soft white paper (natural *maniai* paper from Najio in Hyogo Prefecture is preferred) or cloth.

4. **Netting (twisted fiber, net weave):** The predecessor of nylon, this strong fabric was used in Japan to make both fish nets and pressing sacks (especially the type used to extract soy sauce).
Directions:
Use the kudzu fibers unsplit, and twist them with your fingertips to form a strong twine. Use this as both the warp and woof to weave a 1/8-inch mesh netlike fabric.

6. Kudzu and the Ecosystem

DURING THE past century, the kudzu plant has been used in the United States in a number of unique and creative ways for erosion control, soil improvement, and fodder; it has also served as an ornamental shade plant and a source of honey and wildlife shelter.

The Kudzu Plant

A leguminous perennial vine, kudzu now grows most extensively in the United States but is native to Japan, China, Taiwan, and India.

Varieties

In the United States, *Pueraria lobata* (classified as *P. thunbergiana* until 1947) was the earliest variety introduced and is still the most common. Tropical kudzu (*P. phaseoloides*) was introduced to the U.S. mainland in 1919 but was never naturalized; it was introduced to Puerto Rico as a forage crop in about 1943 and still thrives there. A third variety, *P. tuberosa*, is cultivated in parts of the South.

Japan's most widespread variety of kudzu (*Pueraria lobata*) is called *ma-kudzu* ("true kudzu") and a slightly smaller, less widespread variety (*P. triloba*) is called *himé-kudzu* ("princess kudzu"). A third variety (*P. hirsuta*) is known as "tropical kudzu," and a fourth (*P. tokinensis*) is found only in Okinawa. Kudzu has over ninety regional vernacular names, all of which fall into five basic groups and generally contain various combinations of the characters for "wisteria," "cold," "root," "vine," "bean,". and "kudzu." The approximate English equivalents are: (1) "kudzu wisteria" (*kudzu-fuji, katto, kusho*); (2) "cold root" (*kanné*); (3) "kudzu root" (*kazuné, katsuné*); (4) "vine bean" (*tsuru mamé, kutsu kazura*); and (5) "kudzu vine" (*kutsu kazura*).

In China (and in books about Chinese herbal medicine), kudzu usually bears the scientific name *Pueraria thunbergiana* but may also be listed as *Pachyrhizus thunbergianus*. The popular names for the plant itself are either *ko* ("kudzu") or *katto* ("kudzu wisteria").

Habitat

Although it tends to grow best in semitropical regions, kudzu has a wide climatic range. It thrives in areas with a minimum annual rainfall of 40 inches (it prefers 40 to 60 inches or more) and a long growing season, where the winters are mild (40° to 60°F) and the summers are warm to hot (above 80°F). Because of its large roots, which reach deep into the earth and act as water reservoirs, kudzu can also stand fairly dry climates. It needs irrigation, however, where rainfall is less than 20 inches a year; when irrigated, it even grows reasonably well in relatively arid climates.

An extremely hardy plant, kudzu seems to thrive on almost any type of soil, even in areas where other plants refuse to grow. Tests show that its growth is most rapid on permeable, well-drained loam soils ranging from quite acidic (pH 4.5) to neutral (pH 7.0). It has nevertheless been known to fail on lime soils, on lowlands with a high water table, and in areas with heavy, plastic subsoils.

In Japan kudzu grows wild from northerly Hokkaido (44°N) to the southernmost tip of Kyushu (30°N), a latitude range equivalent to the North American range from southern Maine and central Oregon to northern Florida and Baja California. Kudzu grows abundantly in Japan's mountainous areas up to an elevation of 3,000 feet; it is also found in lowland areas and on many of the small islands. In

Korea, it reportedly grows in areas where the temperature drops to -22°F.

At present kudzu's distribution in North America is generally restricted to the southeastern states, from Florida up to Maryland and southern Pennsylvania, though it has been sighted as well in New York, Illinois, Iowa, and Nebraska. Reports place it as far north as Nova Scotia on the East Coast and Washington on the West; in both of these areas it survives where the winters are mild and the summers cool, but growth is slow and slight (winter temperatures of -25°F kill the roots). Kudzu also grows in scattered parts of South America.

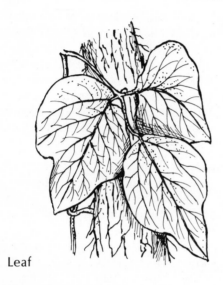
Leaf

Structure and Growth

The young kudzu vine, like its close relative the small soybean plant, has soft brown hairs covering its pliant runners and tendrils. Three to five vines generally grow from the crown of each young root system and spread rapidly over the ground. During the spring and summer, vines in rich soil grow more than a foot a day. A seasonal growth of 50 feet is not unusual, and record growths of 100 feet have been reported. If the vines are deliberately placed on the ground pointed in a certain direction in the spring, they will generally continue to grow in that direction. In dark forests they grow toward the light, often climbing trees in a clockwise spiral and in many cases smothering and killing them after two or three years. Most young vines are about ½ inch in diameter, but one- or two-year-old specimens may reach a diameter of 1 inch and become as hard and woody as most tree branches. Very old vines have been known to reach a diameter of up to 4 inches and as many as thirty may radiate from a single root crown.

During the growing season, the vines produce a dense cover of broad-leafed foliage. The leaves grow in groups of three quite close to the vine on a 4-to-6-inch-long petiole, or leaf stalk. The mature leaf measures about 4 inches across and has a deeply lobed, delicately hairy margin. Kudzu is deciduous, dropping its leaves after the first killing frost in the fall. As many as 250 to 350 leaves may fall within an area of 1 square yard; these, together with dead vines, form a thick layer of absorptive organic material which enriches the soil with humus, reduces run-off, and prevents erosion. Although winter seems to leave the vines lifeless, the leaves return early in the spring, seemingly greener and more vigorous than ever. Several publications mention that kudzu leaves have been made into a breakfast cereal in the United States; however, we have not been able to find the method. The leaves contain the well-known flavoring elements glutamic and butyric acids, as well as asparagin and adenine.

Kudzu establishes new plants by sending down roots at the nodes wherever vines come in contact with the soil. Often spaced at intervals of only 18 inches, the new plants begin to grow immediately, as their roots enlarge, and form new crowns. By the end of the second season, the vine between the crown of the young and old plants usually dies, leaving the new plant on its own. Kudzu has such energy and vitality that, if a cross-sectional disc several inches thick is cut from a large vine or from the roots near its base and is allowed to stand in the open air during the growing season, it will soon begin to send forth strong green shoots. If six hundred cuttings are planted on an acre of bare land, they will completely cover it after two or three years with an almost impenetrable tangle of hip-deep riotous growth.

Root

Kudzu's root system is best compared to that of the potato. The roots usually spread horizontally and in favorable soil generally reach a depth of about 3 feet; in the southern United States some farmers have reported roots penetrating as deep as 8 feet. The pervasive root system contributes to the plant's tenacity, for any root which is not dug or pulled up will continue to grow.

The roots themselves are quite unusual; they swell at various points underground to form fat, tuberous shapes similar in surface texture and appearance to tree roots but having a softer, starchier, and fleshier interior. During the cold months the roots contain a large amount of life-giving starchy material (averaging about 16 percent by weight), which supports plant growth during the early spring and whenever vines are removed by mowing or grazing during the summer. There is no easy way to predict the size of roots merely by looking at the vine; thick, old vines will sometimes have surprisingly small, thin roots, while small vines will occasionally have long, fat ones. A one- or two-year-old vine will generally have roots 1½ to 2 inches in diameter. Older roots achieve diameters of 7 inches and may reach a length of 8 to 10 feet; on rare occasions a 7-foot section, 18 inches in diameter and weighing 200 to 400 pounds, is brought in from the mountains.

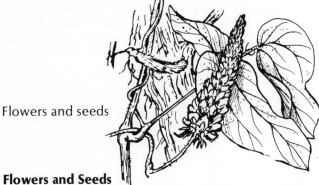

Flowers and seeds

Flowers and Seeds

Kudzu plants first begin to bloom and produce seeds in August and September of their third year. The blossoms are sparse the first season but increase every year. Eventually the kudzu plant (renowned in Japan as one of the "Seven Autumn Flowers") brings forth a long raceme or cluster of purple blossoms shaped like pea flowers or tiny (½-inch-long) butterflies, and smelling like Concord grapes. Unless insect damage interferes, the plant then bears flat, papery, beanlike pods, each about 2 inches long and covered with downy hair. (In the United States, however, these seldom contain seeds, and then apparently only when supported on trees, fences, or banks; in these cases, each pod contains several small seeds that mature in the fall.) An acre of kudzu will produce up to 160 pounds (roughly 2½ bushels) of seed under ideal circumstances. Kudzu seed weighs between 50 and 60 pounds per bushel; each pound contains 40,000 to 45,000 seeds. Since these seeds are difficult to sprout, however, most cultivated kudzu is started from vine cuttings or by dividing the roots. The seeds, if gathered, are generally used as a wild food or for livestock fodder.

Planting and Caring for Kudzu

Leaving the pros and cons of planting kudzu for later discussion, let us consider here the basic techniques. Although kudzu is remarkably hardy and prolific once established, it is surprisingly difficult to start a new stand, even with good soil and a favorable climate. The key reasons for failure are inadequate soil preparation, poor planting stock, improper planting, or insufficient cultivation during the first year.

Soil Preparation and Spacing

If kudzu is to be planted on cultivatable land, the soil should be prepared in the fall or early winter. Use a disc or plow to break a strip 5 to 6 feet wide along the contour rows in which kudzu is to be planted; make sure the soil is loosened to a depth of 6 to 12 inches, especially in hard clay or heavy compact soils. Lay a deep furrow at the center of the strip.

The closer kudzu is spaced, the more quickly it will cover the area. At least 500 plants per acre should be planted (this is equivalent to about 87 square feet per plant); for faster coverage, however, 1,000 plants per acre may be used with a spacing of 12 feet between rows and 3½ to 4 feet between plants in each row. This spacing allows a single-row crop (such as corn or soybeans) to be planted between the rows during the first year. For longer-term intercropping with multiple rows of crops, a spacing of 25 feet between rows is preferred.

In steeply sloping areas (embankments, gullies, dams, etc.), plants should be set in holes 12 to 18 inches in diameter and 12 to 15 inches deep, dug at intervals of 5 to 10 feet. The soil around each hole should be lightly cultivated. These preparations help the primary root system penetrate to depths of 3 feet or more (thereby enabling the plant to resist drought) and facilitate the establishment of new plants at points where the vines touch the ground and send down roots.

Fertilizer Treatment

Tests show that fertilized plants mature much faster and are hardier than their unfertilized counterparts, and on severely eroded or nutrient-poor land or in deep, sandy soils, the use of manure and phosphates is particularly helpful in ensuring rapid ground coverage to check further erosion.

For large-scale application and 12-foot row spacing, 2 to 4 tons of manure and 400 pounds of superphosphate (as a legume, kudzu is particularly responsive to phosphates) should be used per acre before the first planting. If a standard NPK mineral fertilizer is to be used, lime the land to a pH of 6.0 to 6.5 and use 500 pounds of a mixture such as 0-20-20 or its equivalent. Apply minerals in March if no interplanting is to be done, or in September or October if crimson clover, ryegrass, or wild winter peas are to be interplanted with the kudzu.

When spot-planting kudzu in holes (see above), place 2 to 3 shovelsful of manure and 1 to 2 pounds of 18 percent superphosphate or its equivalent in the hole, mix with soil, and then fill the hole with soil. After the soil has become firm and the manure has rotted, set two plants in each hole.

In the spring of the second or third growing seasons, just before growth begins, generous amounts of compost and phosphates can be broadcast on the ground or disked in.

Date of Planting

Kudzu should be planted during the dormant season (December to April) when the soil has been prepared and contains ample moisture. The ideal time depends on the latitude: in the South, February and early March are preferred; farther north, late March or early April are considered best. Those who plant according to the position of the planets recommend planting kudzu in Cancer, Scorpio, Pisces, or Taurus.

Planting Stock and Methods

The three basic types of planting stock, listed in order of popularity among agronomists, are crowns dug from established stands, two-year-old vine cuttings, or nursery plants grown from seeds. (Commercial sources of crowns and seeds are given in appendix A.)

A good two-year-old crown

Crowns, or mature root systems from which the vines have been trimmed, can be dug from well-

established kudzu stands at the rate of 10,000 to 15,000 per acre. A good crown has one or more well-developed fleshy roots at least ½ inch in diameter and 6 inches long, and one or more viable buds (preferably moderate-sized rather than very large). In collecting crowns, the attached vines should be cut back to within one or two inches from the crown and the roots cut off smoothly 6 to 8 inches long. During kudzu's dormant season, from December to April, carefully dig up suitable crowns and transport them to the new planting area. Crowns are usually dug with a turnplow run at a depth that will cut the roots approximately 6 inches below the surface; or, if only a few are needed, they may be dug up with a mattock or shovel and trimmed by hand. Attached vines should be cut back to within 1 or 2 inches of the crown. Since crowns are relatively intolerant to drying, heating, or freezing, they should be transplanted as quickly as possible and some moist soil should be kept on the roots at all times. (If the crowns are transplanted in very cold weather, the buds should also be covered with about 2 inches of soil, which can be removed after the danger of a severe freeze has passed.)

Set the crowns into deep furrows or into holes dug with a mattock or shovel in a slightly elevated, well-settled bed (see "Soil Preparation and Spacing"). Place the roots against the vertical side of the furrow or hole and pack the soil around them firmly, leaving the buds level with or slightly below the surface of the soil. The survival rate for crowns is about 80 percent.

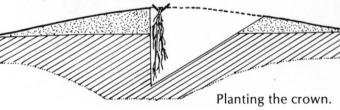

Planting the crown.

Vine Cuttings can be obtained between January and early March from sound vines at least two years old. (Since they are injured by drying, cuttings should be kept moist until they are planted.) The cut section, which should contain at least two nodes and

A two-node vine cutting

measure 5 to 6 feet in length, is set in a deep furrow and covered with 2 to 3 inches of soil so that the top or terminal bud or node is left about 1 inch above the ground.

The survival rate for cuttings thus planted is

about 50 percent. One reason for mortality is that the cut surface, which is rich in protein, often becomes infected by bacteria that cause putrefaction. There are two ways to prevent this. One is the "wave method" of planting long vine cuttings: a series of nodes are left above ground while one, two, or three nodes are buried between them; healthy roots and leaves will grow from the central nodes even if the

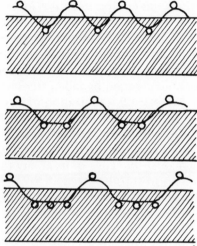

Wave method

ends have begun to decompose. Another method is to tar the upper cut surface; the cutting is then either planted directly or placed in water up to the node and allowed to root. The water is changed daily until ½-inch roots have grown, then the cutting is transplanted to the field and watered well.

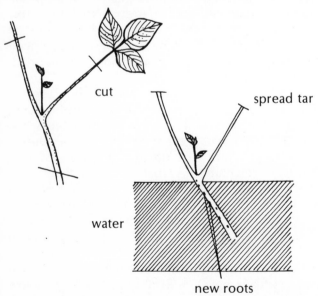

Seeds, originally imported from Japan, are now being developed in the United States and sold commercially. Seeds may also be gathered from mature plants during the fall. These must be scarified to break down the hard seed coat. For small-scale production, the easiest method of scarification is to scratch the seedcoat with a bunch of needles or pins (7 to 8) held in one hand and then to soak the seeds overnight in water. Tests show that 86 percent of seeds thus treated will sprout. (Other means of cracking the seedcoat are: mixing the seeds with fine granite gravel and running them through a rice polishing machine; mixing them with sand and pounding the mixture lightly 20 to 30 times; or soaking them in hot (120°F) water for ten minutes. However, these methods give a sprouting rate of only 20 to 30 percent.) It will require about 15 pounds of seed to plant 1 acre. Under good conditions, 1 pound of seed will produce 3,000 to 4,000 plants.

The seeds should be planted in nursery seedbeds (preferably a level area with sandy or loamy soil that will not bake), following a good rain in May, June, or early July, when the soil is warm and all danger of frosts is past. The soil should be thoroughly prepared. Apply 400 to 600 pounds of a complete NPK fertilizer (such as a 6-8-4) per acre, or 4 to 5 tons of stable manure or rich compost. The fertilizer or manure should be mixed with the soil and bedded on. The beds should be allowed to firm and then "knocked down" until only a low bed is left. Lay off rows 2 feet apart and drill in the scarified seed at the rate of 25 to 30 seeds per linear foot. Cover seeds with about ¼ inch of soil, firm, and moisten. Do not allow the soil to form a crust over the seed. Crusting may be prevented by raking or mulching the soil surface lightly. The plants should be kept shaded in hot, dry weather and carefully cultivated to keep out weeds.

During the late fall or in early spring of the following year, transplant the seedlings in the fields in the same way as crowns. The young vines should be trimmed to within 3 to 5 inches above the ground, and the surrounding ground should be cultivated to control weeds until the plants are large enough to cover the ground.

Cultivation

It is essential that the plants be given clean cultivation during the entire first growing season so that the soil is in good condition for the vines to take root at the nodes. Soil thrown on runners (by shovel or plow) will induce root formation. Weeds should be hoed out of the rows, but it is possible to intercrop, at least in the first season. The cultivated area between the rows may be planted in corn or cotton, for example, and a crop return may be obtained from the land before the kudzu stand is established. If by the second year there is a fair stand of new plants over the entire area between the original rows, there is no need for further cultivation. If the area between the rows is not well covered, it should be plowed back to where the plants are well established, then cultivated and intercropped as in the first year.

Pests and Diseases

Kudzu is seldom bothered by insects or plant diseases, and any damage to its leaves is generally balanced by a prolific production of foliage. It does, however, have certain minor natural enemies. Nematodes cause the condition commonly known as "root knot": these small eel-like worms attack the roots and reduce the plants' vigor, especially during droughts. (Although there have been no reports of kudzu being killed by nematodes, plants dug from infested areas should not be planted elsewhere.) A disease called "blackleg" can be caused by lack of oxygen in the nursery soil; seedling beds should be sterilized as a precaution. The leaves can be affected by a mosaic disease which covers them with white spots and causes shrinking. A rust disease will color the vine and cause it to swell but will not effect the yield of fiber. In Japan kudzu's most serious enemy is the ½-inch-long red fruit bug, which eats the leaves, buds, and seeds, often rendering the plant infertile.

Kudzu for Erosion Control

Kudzu is used on steep road and railroad embankments, slopes, fills, and gullies to prevent erosion and landslides. It works in three basic ways:

1. The thick layer of shed leaves, held in place by the vines and vine roots, protects the soil against beating rainfall and wind, soaks up run-off water, and quickly forms a blanket of absorptive organic humus which heals the land and returns it to fine pasturage. Tests have shown that even very steep slopes, when covered with a natural mulch of frost-killed kudzu leaves, have a water run-off of less than 2 percent. And fast-growing kudzu produces this thick, moisture-retaining mulch in record time.

2. The firm root system at the central crown and numerous vine nodes forms an extensive network which holds the surface soil; the ropelike vines hug the ground and net it down, even when it is subject to large volumes of water flowing at high velocities (as, for instance, in flash floods).

3. The large primary roots anchor the deeper earth firmly, preventing landslides.

Kudzu has numerous advantages over other protective covering crops; it is inexpensive to establish and maintain, fast-growing, and hardy enough to stand even the most unfavorable soil and moisture

conditions (its deep roots enable it to survive even the most extreme droughts, when other ground covers—such as grasses or legumes—would perish). As a perennial, it requires no replanting; its nitrogen-fixing bacteria and fallen leaves actually enrich and restore the soil; and it is more attractive than concrete retaining walls and other man-made embankments.

For three particular soil erosion problems, kudzu has virtually no competitors. It is ideal for: (1) control of newly cut channels—because of its rapid growth, freedom from maintenance, ability to prevent tree growth, and inability to grow on the water surface (thus, channel banks are stabilized and unlikely to become clogged by fallen trees or plants growing in the water); (2) stabilization of steep road cuts—because of its rapid establishment, deep-rootedness, and clinging viny tendrils; and (3) coverage of mine spoils and denuded areas that will not support other plants—because of its ability to flourish on even the poorest soils.

It is also used to prevent erosion under four other, more general types of conditions:

1. *Cultivated Land:* Eroded farms that have become a wasteland, their topsoil washed away and their surface gouged with deep gullies, can be restored to rich and verdant farmland after several years of planting in kudzu. There are countless examples of farms in the Deep South which, although their soil was so bad that it would support no other protective vegetation, were saved by kudzu. Kudzu is generally countour-planted in strips on sloping land or cultivated on every third terrace; row crops are grown on the intermediate strips or terraces. Kudzu can also be used to stabilize uncultivable slopes of 15 percent or more, within or adjoining crop fields.

2. *Dams, Riverbanks, and Water-Disposal Systems:* When used to strengthen earthfill dams, kudzu's deep roots reinforce the infrastructure while the vines and leaves prevent surface erosion. (During the 1940s, 1 ton of wild kudzu plants was sent from Nagano Prefecture in Japan to strengthen dams along the Yellow River in China.) When planted along eroding riverbanks, the strong vines will not tear, even at times of heavy flooding. In designing a water run-off system from terraced farmland, kudzu can be used to line the meadow outlets to prevent gullying, and gullies can be stabilized with kudzu and gradually developed into satisfactory meadow outlets by plowing the banks down each spring until the gullies are filled and a smooth mowing surface has been formed. A strip of kudzu 15 or 20 feet wide immediately above a diversion channel will filter out

coarse silt and thus prevent the channel from filling and becoming ineffective; the vines cover the channel bottom and prevent erosion. Moreover, a ground cover of kudzu restores dried-up springs and ponds, and nearby streams soon run clear, because kudzu so perfectly prevents water loss and silting.

3. *Embankments and Fills:* The U.S. Government publication *Kudzu for Erosion Control in the Southeast* states that:

Kudzu can be established more cheaply on highway banks than most other types of vegetation used. One row along the top of the bank will, if properly prepared, fertilized, planted, and cultivated, cover the road bank and ditch with a dense growth of vines and completely control erosion within 2 or 3 years. This type of planting is much less expensive than sodding with grass. Kudzu has the further advantage that it requires less bank sloping than is necessary where grass is planted. Kudzu has also been used successfully by a number or railroads for the protection of fill banks against erosion . . . on slopes of as much as 70 percent.

4. *Gulley Control:* Small gullies not only cut across fields, making them impossible to cultivate, but also transport silt and gravel to lowland farms and streams; in streams this can cause overflow of floodwater and reduce the water storage capacity of reservoirs. One solution is to build low brush dams across the tops of gullies and to plant kudzu in the silt that is deposited above the dams, then fertilize it well with compost (or manure) and phosphates. Where gullies are 50 feet or more apart, it is advisable to plant kudzu in the areas between them, spacing the holes 20 feet apart and arranging them in rows on the contour so that they may be cultivated with a plow. Dig holes to 18 inches in diameter and 12 to 14 inches deep, apply 2 to 3 shovelsful of compost or manure and 1 to 2 pounds of organic phosphate in the bottom of each hole, mix well with soil, and fill the hole with soil. Water liberally, set two plants in each hole, then pack firmly and give sufficient cultivation to control grass and weeds.

For large caving gullies, some plants should be started in the caved-in material in the gulley bottoms and one to three rows planted parallel to the rim. The first row may be 6 to 8 feet from the edge of the gulley and other rows about 10 feet apart. Even after dropping into the gulley when the ground caves in, these plants will continue to grow; eventually the bottom and sides of the gulley will be completely stabilized.

Kudzu for Soil Improvement

Kudzu may play an integral part in soil building and/or land reclamation programs by contributing in at least six basic areas:

1. *Adding Organic Leaf Matter:* When kudzu drops its large, delicate leaves in the fall, they make a thick layer of flaky leaf mold that feels like a mattress underfoot and covers the ground completely. This leaf mold enters the earth as organic matter, lightens topsoil, and restores to fertility even the most exhausted soils, while reducing loss of plant food due to leaching. After three to five years, enough new topsoil will have been created to support farm crops after the kudzu is harvested. The leaf mold also serves to retain moisture and keep the soil cool (on days when the surface temperature of exposed soil is 140°F, it will be about 89°F under the leaf mold). These conditions are conducive to the growth of underground bacteria which give life to the soil.

2. *Fixing Nitrogen:* Like alfalfa and soybeans, kudzu is a legume that hosts nitrogen-fixing bacteria on its roots; these bacteria capture nitrogen (one of the three key elements in all fertilizers) from the air and fix it in the soil, thereby greatly enhancing the soil's fertility. In Japan, the effectiveness of this long-lasting, free organic fertilizer has been recognized for centuries. Farmers have found that when they clear land overgrown in kudzu (and pull out the roots), then plant food crops, the crops grow prolifically even without the use of additional fertilizer. When mountain forests are sold for timber, land with kudzu on it is of greater value, since the nitrogen it fixes stimulates the trees' growth.

3. *"Green Manure"* (cover crops plowed into the soil in order to enrich it): Kudzu foliage is rich in calcium and contains more of the essential NPK components (nitrogen, 0.70; phosphoric acid, 0.16; potassium, 0.45) than even red clover (0.48, 0.09, 0.37, respectively), which is widely viewed as one of the finest cover crops. Moreover, the green manure values per acre of kudzu is 2.9 times that of alfalfa. At the U.S. Department of Agriculture experimental station in Auburn, Alabama, a field of kudzu was planted and turned under after three years. During the next ten years, four crops of corn, seven of oats, and two of sorghum were grown on this field. The ten-year average yield of corn was 2.3 times as great as that for a control plot; the oat yield was 1.5 times and the sorghum yield 1.8 times as great as the control. Even ten years after the kudzu had been turned under, the kudzu plot produced an average of 9.2 more bushels per acre than an adjacent plot where no kudzu had been grown. This dramatic yield

increase was thought to be the result of both the "green manure" and nitrogen fixation.

• = permanent kudzu plants   ○ = wheat
x = kudzu to be uprooted before third year

4. *Intercropping:* Kudzu is useful for intercropping for two reasons: (1) it enriches the soil with nitrogen, and (2) it lies dormant during the winter (October to March). The kudzu vines may be cut any time after the middle of August and the ground between the rows prepared for cold season crops such as winter wheat, barley, sorghum, sunflower seeds, or millet. Generally, the winter crop should be planted in double rows with a 3-foot space between each double row; kudzu is planted in the middle of this space at intervals of 5 feet, to be increased to 20 feet by thinning before the third year. Also, after the winter crop is harvested in the late winter or early spring, a warm-weather crop, usually corn or cotton, may be planted between the kudzu rows. In the United States, where warm weather intercropping with corn is most popular, a much wider spacing between kudzu rows is recommended to prevent the new kudzu vines from interfering with the row crop: 25 feet between rows and 3½ feet between kudzu plants in each row. Reports from U.S. agricultural research stations show that corn intercropped with kudzu produces average yields over 200 percent larger than normal, and some farms have shown increases of 400 to 700 percent, accompanied by greatly decreased fertilizer requirements.

Most orchard trees do not begin to bear fruit until four to five years after planting, and forest trees such as pine and cedar take even longer to mature. If these trees are intercropped with kudzu, their growth is accelerated, and the foliage harvested from the vines each fall can serve as a major source of livestock fodder or mulch. Vines moving toward trees should be redirected, and those which have begun to climb should be cut and used as mulch. In Latin America, some farmers grow kudzu among their coffee shrubs; apparently the vines do not climb the shrubs.

5. *Land Reclamation:* Kudzu may be used to reclaim semidesert areas or land overgrown in weeds. Any semidesert land that has enough moisture to support other types of vegetation will probably support kudzu. To start the plants, a large bamboo pipe about 20 inches long and 4½ inches in diameter with its nodes pierced and removed is filled with moistened soil, and a kudzu seedling is planted in it. The pipe is buried upright in the desert and, if possible, watered occasionally. Initial application of fertilizer will aid growth, but once the plant is established, it will enrich the soil with organic leaf matter and nitrogen. By the time the pipe rots, a year or two later, the roots will have gone deep into the earth.

Kudzu also effectively competes with weeds. In forests throughout Borneo, Sumatra, Indonesia, and other parts of Southeast Asia where slash-and-burn agriculture (or defoliation) has been practiced, the land has often been left denuded until it has become overgrown with weeds. Kudzu planted in such areas has helped to control or eradicate weeds while enriching the soil.

6. *Compost and Mulch:* Kudzu foliage and vines are known to make excellent compost in a relatively short time. For best results, run the material through a shredder, pile it in layers with manure, watering each layer to the dampness of a well-wrung sponge, and cover with burlap sacking or plastic sheeting. Shredded matter turned every two weeks will be ready in six to eight weeks. Even if not shredded, the vines will disintegrate quickly and be transformed into rich dark compost in four to six months.

Kudzu leaves and small vines, used whole or shredded, make a mulch equal in value to that made with alfalfa. Spread in a thick layer in gardens and orchards, it prevents weed growth (thereby saving work and eliminating the need for herbicides), slowly adds rich humus, keeps soil cool and moist (thereby saving water), stimulates the growth of earthworms and beneficial bacteria, and prevents erosion. Mulch in the spring, once the soil is warm and the plants are thriving.

Kudzu as Fodder

Since it is a perennial and does not have to be planted each year, kudzu serves as a very low-cost source of fodder once it has been established. On small farms and homesteads where high-quality fodder is expensive or difficult to obtain, kudzu can make a major contribution. Animals can graze on the live plants or the vines may be cut, cured, and dried for hay. Cattle, hogs, chickens, goats, sheep, horses, and rabbits reportedly like both fresh and dried kudzu, often preferring it to grass or commercial hay, and kudzu is said to improve livestock health.

The main source of fodder is the leaves, which constitute roughly 50 percent of the hay by weight (the rest being stems and woody vines); the vines, however, if shredded, may actually serve as a rich source of carbohydrates. Rich in protein (up to 18%), calcium, vitamin A (carotene), and vitamin D (see table 2), kudzu ranks equal to clover and alfalfa in nutritional value (however, if kudzu is grown on acidic soils, its calcium content may be lower than that of alfalfa. Since kudzu's long roots will penetrate beneath farmed-out surface soil, it can send minerals up to the leaves, which, when dried, are 92 percent as digestible as red clover.

Grazing

Kudzu has the advantage of furnishing considerable grazing through the fall and into the winter; livestock have been seen grazing frosted leaves in preference to green oats as late as the first of February. And in times of drought, kudzu has frequently enabled livestock to survive the summer. Kudzu is best used for grazing in late July, August, and September: too early grazing reduces the plant's vitality, and overgrazing can severly damage or even kill mature stands.

Before being grazed, kudzu should be allowed to establish a thick stand; this is usually not produced before the third year. It may then be over-sown with such plants as fescue grass, oats, ryegrass, crimson clover, or tall fescue. Mixed planting of crimson clover or winter peas with ryegrass is also recommended. This will furnish winter grazing and extend the grazing period over a large portion of the year, since most of these crops can be grazed from late fall until mid-April. In Japan, mountains covered with wild kudzu are sold for use as fodder, and ancient records from Wakayama Prefecture show that kudzu, then used as a horse fodder, was once collected in lieu of taxes.

Kudzu is excellent for grazing cattle; allot one acre per head. In an average 68-day season, a typical cow will gain 128 pounds and a steer 237 pounds. Beef cows will carry calves longer, and the calves will also gain weight on the grazing. Dairy cows will increase in milk from summer pasture to kudzu grazing because of the high protein content of the leaves.

Hogs do extremely well on kudzu grazing. They like the fleshy roots, which they are fond of rooting up unless rings are placed in their noses. One acre will carry four to six mature hogs. It will partially replace their protein supplements but will not fatten them if no other feed is supplied.

Kudzu is also excellent for poultry, either hand-fed dry or as a grazing crop from May until frost. One acre will support two hundred birds.

Hay

Kudzu makes an excellent hay which cures easily. Before mowing is begun, the stand should be well established, completely covering the ground, and about knee-high. It usually takes at least two full seasons on good soil and three to five seasons on poor soils (unless the kudzu is fertilized) before the kudzu is ready to cut. Two cuttings per year, one in July and another in October, give the best quality hay; cutting is also easier since the vines don't get too large and tough. More than two cuttings a year will damage the stand and, if repeated, kill it. If only one cutting is made, this should be in July or early August.

Kudzu's viny nature makes mechanical har-

Table 2: Composition of Nutrients in Kudzu Fodder

	Moisture Percent	Protein Percent	Fat Percent	Sugars Percent	Fiber Percent	Ash Percent	Vit. A Mg	Vit. C Mg
Fresh leaves	76.9	4.0	0.6	10.2	6.8	1.5	3.0	3.6
Dry Leaves	7.1	16.1	2.5	40.7	27.5	6.1		
Meal	7.1	21.2	3.3	53.8	7.5	8.1		
Cured Hay	5.3	11.3	2.2	39.2	35.1	6.9		

Source: *Kuzu: The Plant to Save Japan*

vesting difficult. For best results use an iron rider bar attached to the end of a cutter bar, which divides and frees the vines as the swath is cut.

American farmers report harvesting an average of 5600 pounds (2.7 tons) of hay per acre, while Japanese researchers show the following figures in pounds per acre: fresh kudzu leaves, 9,924; alfalfa, 5,789; clover, 4,962; dry kudzu leaves, 2,894; fiber-free kudzu meal, 2,315, and green cut soybean leaves, 2,232.

In good hay-curing weather (warm and dry), kudzu will cure in 2 days. The hay should be cut when both ground and kudzu are dry, left in the swath for a few hours, and then put in windrows. The next morning, once the dew is off, the windrows should be turned. That afternoon the hay should be baled or put into the barn. When the growth is very rank, the kudzu may be forked instead of raked.

Good silage can also be made from kudzu by mixing it with grass so that the mixture contains 60 percent moisture. The total moisture content of kudzu at the time of cutting is about 75 percent; therefore, it must be handled as rapidly as possible.

In Japan dried kudzu leaves are occasionally ground and the fibers removed to make a meal, which may be mixed with other feeds or compressed to form granular pellets.

Kudzu as an Ornamental Shade Plant

One of kudzu's first uses in the United States was as an ornamental shade plant. In Francis Howard's *Landscaping with Vines* (Macmillan, 1959) a full page is devoted to this subject, and kudzu is listed for the same purpose in some seed and nursery catalogs. A kudzu vine in full bloom is indeed a beautiful addition to the landscape and the cut flowers make attractive miniature arrangements. If the vines are trellised, there is no danger of the plant spreading via roots from the vine nodes. Provide a tall, sturdy lattice support. Tip-prune during the growing season to keep the plant from becoming woody and rangy, and cut back hard each fall, retaining some of the old wood, since the plant blooms on the previous season's growth.

Kudzu for Honeybees and Wildlife

Honey collected from bees frequenting kudzu blossoms is said to be of the highest quality, with a delightful fragrance and flavor. Brazil is reported to have recently imported kudzu plants for use primarily as a honey source.

Kudzu thickets also provide excellent cover for many types of wildlife. And there is a well-known saying in the South that "snakes don't get in the kudzu because it tickles them." A contradictory proverb, however, states that green snakes love kudzu.

To Plant or Not To Plant

It would be irresponsible to discuss kudzu's role in the ecosystem without mentioning the possible long-range problems that might arise from kudzu planting and cultivation. It must be stated clearly at this point that the great majority of farmers in the United States who have kudzu growing on their land (as well as a fairly large percentage in Japan) consider the plant to be a pernicious pest which they would like to see totally eradicated. Although they acknowledge its numerous virtues, they feel that the difficulty of controlling its growth greatly overrides all other considerations.

In early 1976, when *Organic Gardening and Farming Magazine* invited its readers to send in information about their experiences with the plant, most of the letters described kudzu as being much more trouble than it is worth:

You want letters about kudzu? Here's one from a confirmed kudzu hater . . . Driving along the highways and roads here is heartbreaking—dead trees everywhere, smothered by kudzu. In the summer, nearly everything in sight is covered by green kudzu foliage (deserted houses, trees, bushes, farm equipment, hills, road banks) and a terrible tangle of vines. Oh yes, we have it on our property. You can't walk where it grows; its so thick that snakes are invisible until stepped on. When firmly entrenched, as it is here, constant cutting, plowing under, and burning are ineffective except to keep it from spreading. In spite of frequent clipping, it still manages to climb the trees — not just up the trunks but, incredibly, 5 to 6 feet straight up to limbs some distance from the trunk.

It's extremely hard to cut when green because of its great elasticity of fibers and fibrosity. It's not possible to cut it with a lawn mower and sickle mowers and even "bush hogs" (large tractor-operated rotary mowers) get hopelessly clogged or entangled in its thick, tough vines. I know one neighbor who claims to have buried a pile of ripped-up kudzu under 10 feet of earth only to have it come out after two years.

I hope someone writes in to say how it

can be killed. We're getting desperate, since it spreads not only on the ground but from treetop to treetop. I would hate for anyone to unknowingly plant this monstrosity and then be unable to get rid of it without drastic poisoning.

W. F.
Mississippi

My husband and I have vivid childhood memories of kudzu vines literally taking over large sections of woodlands and fields in Maryland and Tennessee, and it became quite a curse to us when it started creeping across our own fields.

We feel the potential ability this perennial has for getting out of control outweighs any of its desirable qualities and therefore advise against its use.

E. M.
Plainfield, New Hampshire

Plant kudzu? No! No! For heaven's sake no!

M. T.
Virginia

In my experience, this is a pest plant without parallel. It got started in our neighborhood four years ago and has spread to four lots already in spite of herculean efforts on our part. We have tried tractors, plows, disc harrows, hand tools, and three different herbicides so far.

I know that I must destroy part of my land in order to save the rest of it. I will forgive the chemical companies of their many sins if they will invent an herbicide for kudzu. This is a land destroyer—not a soil builder. Kudzu is like a cancer.

It is heartbreaking to realize that I am fighting a losing battle. I am 65 years old and don't have the energy to dig 6-foot-deep-holes to remove the kudzu roots. Unless chemicals can do the job, my garden will eventually be gone.

W. M. C.
South Carolina

I would not recommend planting kudzu under any circumstances. We have had a two-year battle with this plant and if we had a dollar for every hour spent in cutting kudzu vines and pulling kudzu roots, we would be quite wealthy. The best preventative is to have never planted it in the first place.

H. M.
Alabama

To the best of our knowledge, very little kudzu is now being planted in America, even in the Deep South, except on embankments for erosion control. Anyone visiting local agricultural offices in search of information is apt to be roundly cursed, then told with pride that the pest is now under control and that all of the old brochures have been thrown out.

Likewise, virtually no cultivation is practiced on farms in Japan today. Like their American counterparts, Japanese farmers point out that the harvesting of roots and vines, which is difficult to do even with farm machinery, is hard, slow work, and they are reluctant to plant for fear that kudzu will get out of control, smothering neighboring trees and crops. Three additional reasons are also mentioned: (1) there are an estimated 220,000 acres of wild crop available for harvest at little or no land use cost; (2) farmland, which constitutes only 16 percent of the country's total surface area, is extremely valuable and when planted in other basic food crops returns a larger profit unless all of kudzu's components—root starch, leaf fodder (or hay) and chlorophyll, vine and root fiber—are harvested and sold; and (3) seedlings and seeds are not readily available.

Nevertheless, kudzu is widely cultivated on embankments and erosion gullies in Japan, and scholars such as Mukaeda Toshio in his *Kuzu; The Plant to Save Japan*, argue that it should be cultivated much more widely on the thousands of acres of hillside land unsuitable for other crops; he recommends that the foliage be used for fodder.

In Korea, the situation is quite different: new kudzu farms are being established each year and can be seen for mile after mile as one travels by train or car. The plants are used in most of the ways described in this chapter, and the root starch is extracted to make kudzu powder which is used in local cuisine or exported to Japan.

We feel that the negative image kudzu has in America could be improved if three factors were to change:

1. *If the same price were offered for kudzu roots in America that is now being offered in Japan.* A step in this direction will be taken as soon as the first shops making kudzu powder are started in America.

2. *If livestock farmers were to stop using corn, soybeans, oats, and wheat as fodder,* either in sym-

pathy for the millions of people starving to death for lack of these foods or because human demand for them makes their prices exorbitant. The growing world food crisis is already pressuring farmers to look for alternate fodders.

3. *If modern society were to reconsider the advantages of traditional organic agriculture.* The emerging ecological awareness of the dangers presented by agrichemicals may be a start.

Granting the possibility of a new trend, the key to the financially successful cultivation of kudzu would lie in using all of its basic by-products in an integrated way. Although the most valuable material (at least potentially in America) is the root starch, the fodder (from leaves, roots, and vines), the fiber (from vines and roots), the chlorophyll (from leaves), and the tannin (from roots and vines) could also serve as supplementary sources of income.

Controlling and Eradicating Kudzu

We feel that the dangers have been overestimated. In most parts of the United States (except for the Deep South), the relatively cold climate, low rainfall, and/or short growing season will serve naturally to control kudzu growth. Even under conditions conducive to growth, small stands may be contained by turning back the runners, and large stands that threaten to encroach on fields or forests can be contained by making a trip along the border of the kudzu three or four times each season with a harrow or a plow to drag the runners back into the kudzu; in some cases, paved roads act as effective barriers. Finally, large stands on level pasture land may be easily controlled by regular mowing or grazing, followed by disking and plowing during the winter.

There at least four ways to eradicate kudzu, listed here in order of our preference. We recommend the first three, which are ecologically sound.

1. *Overgrazing:* Allow continuous, close grazing by a large number of animals for two or three seasons. For quicker results, plow each season.

2. *Burning, Mowing, and Plowing:* This method allows eradication in one season. Burn kudzu in the fall, then mow closely at the beginning of the growing season (April); repeat at least three times during the summer. Finally disk and plow deeply during the next fall or winter. This method also works if the burning is omitted.

3. *Digging up the Roots:* Use picks and shovels or a backhoe. This method takes a great deal of time and effort, but the roots can be sold or processed.

4. *Applying Chemicals:* This method, which is extremely hard on the environment, should be used only in forest areas and on highway embankments, or as a last resort. The three most effective kudzu herbicides listed by trade name (with common name in parentheses) in order of effectiveness are Tordon (ticloran; made by Dow), Banvel (dicamba), and Maintain (chlorflurenol). Other recommended herbicides include Silvex and 2, 4, 5-T, and 2-4-D. The quickest way to eradicate kudzu is to burn it in the fall, then plow the land and have a distributor behind the tractor with which to spread 50 pounds of Tordon pellets per acre of land; this method eradicates kudzu in one year. Or the pellets can be broadcast with a "belly grinder" cyclone seeder in live kudzu, but eradication then takes two years and requires several treatments. Some grasses may be grown starting six months after application but broadleaf plants must wait one to two years.

Japanese crest, kudzu leaf

Appendix A. Real Kudzu Powder and Its Imitations

In Japan not all of the products in stores labeled as "kudzu powder" actually contain the real thing. Some contain an inexpensive potato starch that resembles kudzu powder, while others contain a mixture of real kudzu powder and potato starch. Likewise, most "kudzu noodles" (see chapter 2) contain either this mixture or no real kudzu powder at all. The most common imitations of kudzu powder are sweet-potato starch (kansho or Satsuma denpun) and Irish potato starch (bareisho denpun). Most of the kudzu powder sold in the United States at natural food stores has been carefully monitored by both its Japanese exporter and the stateside distributor, so that customers may generally rest assured that they are buying the authentic product. However, some of the low-cost starch labeled as "kudzu" and sold at Japanese grocery markets has been found, upon analysis, to contain only potato starch (at least one large natural food dealer in Europe reports receiving kudzu powder of dubious authenticity). Because of this confusing and unfortunate situation, Japanese consumers have begun to use the expression "real kudzu powder" (*hon-kudzu*) in much the same way that we in the West say "real butter."

The first and primary cause of the deliberate deception involved lies in Japan's hopelessly outdated labeling laws, which are the result of collusion between the food industry and the government's ruling party. The use of chemical additives and the practice of misleading labeling is now so widespread that the food industry fears a firm set of labeling laws would cause a crisis leading to a major loss of consumer confidence. Thus, Japan remains the only major industrial country in the world where many foods are sold without their ingredients clearly stated. We would like to see the introduction of a law specifying that any package bearing the label "kudzu" must contain only 100 percent real kudzu powder. Conscientious merchandizers might be encouraged to add the phrase "Contains no other starches or additives." Mixtures of kudzu powder and other starches would be labeled thus both in the main title and in the ingredients listing in which components are listed in order of percentage by weight. Such practices would not only protect the consumer but encourage conscientious makers to produce a pure, natural product without fear of being undersold by cheap imitations.

A second cause of the problem is dishonesty—or disinterest—on the part of most Japanese producers and distributors of kudzu powder. In the trade all kudzu products and grades are divided into two basic types: hon-kudzu ("real kudzu") and *nami-kudzu*, which can refer either to potato starches processed in the same way as kudzu powder or to a mixture of real kudzu powder and these starches. (The very term "nami-kudzu" is itself misleading, since it refers to two widely different products which sell for different prices.) In practice, the commercial mixtures generally contain from 15 to 50 percent real kudzu (see appendix B), but the amount is rarely if ever marked on the package. Producers generally tell their distributors what percent of real kudzu powder is contained in their nami-kudzu, but the distributors rarely tell the retail stores, confectionery shops, or individual consumers to whom they sell. When retailers buy in bulk, generally they are simply given a sheet listing brand names and prices; products almost never list ingredients. Thus, buyers purchasing the less expensive varieties have no way of knowing whether they are getting an inferior grade of hon-kudzu or an adulterated mixture. Actually, nami-kudzu, when by this is meant 100 percent potato starch, can actually be a higher-quality product than mass-produced potato starch, since the former is still processed and dried in the same slow, traditional way as real kudzu powder, using only the finest natural ingredients and none of the chemical additives used in most commercial potato starches. Nami-kudzu mixtures are usually made with undried potato starch purchased in October or November, stored until the kudzu harvesting season begins, and then mixed with low-quality kudzu powder—the rather dark kudzu starch that settles after the kudzu starch has been washed for the third or fourth time, or an inferior Korean import. During the mixing, there is some separation of the kudzu and potato starches since the latter is heavier, but the difference is slight. The final product may have much the same appearance and texture as real kudzu powder, but cuisine prepared with it will have an inferior consistency and flavor, and, of course, will lack the precious medicinal properties. Moreover, since both the dark kudzu starch and the Korean import can both be sold as "real kudzu," it is often not clear to buyers whether they have purchased a low-priced high-quality real kudzu, an inferior grade of real kudzu, or a high-priced nami-kudzu mixture. The problem is further complicated by the fact that at least one maker of kudzu powder in Kyushu sells its products under the prestigious name "Yoshino Kudzu," even though Yoshino is located almost 1,000 miles away.

A third cause of the problem is that, as kudzu powder was Japan's earliest thickening and jelling agent, the word gradually came to be used in a generic sense. In modern times this linguistic habit has come to have unfortunate consequences.

A fourth cause of the problem is that the average Japanese consumer, no longer clearly understanding why real kudzu powder is superior to its low cost competitors as a medicine, health food, and ingredient in cuisine, hesitates to pay the higher price. As a home remedy, kudzu is quickly being replaced by pills and chemical preparations, and it is sold in fewer and fewer neighborhood grocery stores. Its last retail stronghold in Japan is the natural food stores, increasingly popular in recent years. Yet neither the word "kudzu powder" nor the foods and natural medicines made from it are nearly as well known today as they were before World War II. And for much of the younger generation, "kudzu" is an altogether unfamiliar term.

A fifth and decisive cause lies in the very large price difference that has emerged between kudzu and related starches. Many producers of kudzu powder now feel that they must sell a mixed or adulterated product in order to stay competitive. The price of real kudzu powder has risen at a steady and often rather rapid rate, while that of the potato starches has actually fallen, as a result of the economies of mass production and recent technological advances. Consequently, production of kudzu powder has slowly fallen while that of its competitors has increased. In 1975, according to official government statistics, Japan produced 180,000 (short) tons of Irish potato starch plus 100,000 tons of sweet-potato starch. In addition, the country imported 679,000 tons of cornstarch and 83,000 tons of wheat starch, amounting to a total national consumption of 1.2 million tons. Kudzu powder represents such a small percentage of this total that official figures are no longer kept. Estimates place total annual production of real kudzu powder today at about 450 tons, or roughly 0.1 percent of the domestic potato starch production and .03 percent of the total starch consumption.

High-quality, naturally processed kudzu powder is expensive because its raw materials are difficult to obtain, production is on a relatively small scale requiring a great deal of hand-work and time, and can only be done during the cold part of each year. Moreover, 100 pounds of freshly cut roots yield only about 6 pounds of high-quality, dry kudzu powder. By comparison, sweet potatoes and Irish potatoes are easily grown and harvested; the starch can be extracted and refined in about three days, using a largely automated process; the yield is close to 20 percent. Consequently, in Japan, the retail and wholesale prices of kudzu powder are generally about ten times as high per unit weight as those for the potato starches.

Prices for kudzu powder differ quite widely from maker to maker and depend on the quality of the product, the scale of production, and, in the case of adulterated mixtures, the percentage of real kudzu powder they contain. Kudzu made in Yoshino (see appendix B) is sometimes said to be of higher quality than that made in warmer regions to the south, since the colder weather minimizes fermentation of the starch during processing. Yoshino makers are generally fairly small and many import their raw ingredients from Kyushu, both of which lead to higher prices.

In 1977 in Japan, producers sold real kudzu powder in 11-pound cartons for about 12 cents (U.S.) per ounce; wholesalers for 13—17 cents per ounce; and retailers for 25—32 cents per ounce (in 4-ounce packages). (Comparable prices for nami-kudzu were 3 cents from the producer, 4 cents wholesale, and 12—21 cents retail.) Japanese exporters sold their product to natural foods distributors in the West for 11—13 cents per ounce, and it generally retailed for 40—43 cents per ounce. The fact that the price increases by 50 percent during the import process might encourage Americans to get into production.

How can you tell whether or not the kudzu you are buying is real kudzu powder, potato starch processed like the real powder, or a mixture of the two? Real kudzu powder comes in chunks, whereas pure potato starch comes as a white powder, but as far as the rest go, by far the best way is to buy a reliable brand from a reputable company which sells its product in packages that are clearly labeled. Likewise, wholesalers should demand that producers or exporters provide them with a written guarantee of the kudzu powder's authenticity, along with a certified laboratory test.

Generally, real kudzu powder retails for a higher price than imitation or adulterated products, but not always. In 1975, for example, a major Japanese natural food distributor picked seven products labeled "kudzu powder" at random from Japanese natural food stores and supermarkets and subjected them to laboratory microscopic analysis. Only two of the seven were shown to be 100 percent real kudzu powder; four were pure potato starch, and one was a mixture containing equal parts real kudzu powder and potato starch. Interestingly enough, the prices of the potato starches ranged from 126 percent to 48 percent the price of the real kudzu powder.

The most accurate way to test for real kudzu powder is to do a microscopic analysis. Kudzu powder is seen to have a distinctly crystalline grain structure with numerous plane surfaces meeting at clearly defined angles, whereas the grains of potato starches are considerably larger and have a round or oval shape.

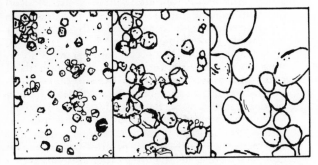

The size and shapes of different kudzu-like products are shown in figure above. The left-hand frame shows real kudzu powder with a grain size of 2 to 8 microns and a relatively small range of variation. The central frame shows sweet-potato starch with a grain size of 5 to 30 microns and a wide range of sizes. And the third frame shows Irish potato starch with a grain size of 20 to 50 microns. Japanese healers point out that kudzu powder's small grain size is another expression of its basically compact *yang* nature.

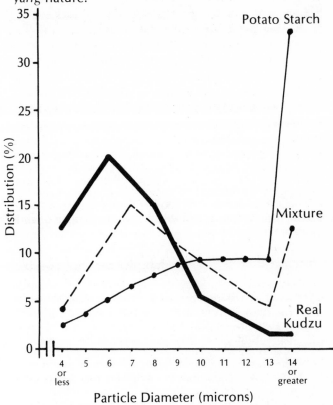

Particle Diameter (microns)

When particle sizes of real kudzu powder, potato starches, and a mixture of the two are compared, we note that for the real powder, the most abundant particle size is about 6 microns, whereas for potato starches it is greater than 14 microns (data provided by Muso Shokuhin in Japan). Although no similar studies are available for arrowroot, it is believed to have a grain size midway between that of real kudzu powder and sweet-potato starch.

Appendix B. Institutions and People Connected with Kudzu

SHOPS MAKING KUDZU POWDER IN JAPAN

Japan's five foremost producers of commercial kudzu powder are listed here in order of output of real kudzu (see appendix A). Most have had their kudzu powder exported to the West. A number of other small shops are thought to be located in remote mountain villages of Niigata, Fukushima, and Nara Prefectures, but their product is not readily available and we have been unable to obtain their addresses.

Hiro Hachido Shoten, Nikawa 555-1, Ushine, Tarumi-shi, Kagoshima-ken, Kyushu 899-46. Tel: 09943-6-2010. Mr. Makoto Taguchi, director. Located in the small town of Ushine across the bay from Kagoshima in southern Kyushu, at the foot of seemingly endless mountains covered with wild kudzu vines, this company has been in the Taguchi family for 15 years; it was founded to supply kudzu powder to the lord of the great Kuroda fief. The present factory was built in 1947 and, after numerous enlargements, reached its full size in 1970.

Hiro Hachido is best known for its large output and reasonable prices, its unique combination of traditional and modern production methods, and its exclusive contracts with Mitoku and Muso Shokuhin, Japan's largest exporters of natural foods. Employing 45 workers in the factory itself and another 150 workers to harvest the wild kudzu roots, Hiro Hachido produces about 330,000 pounds of real kudzu powder each year, sold under the brand name "Hiro Hachido Kudzu," plus an additional 600,000 pounds of another product sold as "Yamato Kudzu" which actually contains only sweet potato-starch (*kansho denpun*). The former is sold primarily to natural food stores; the latter to Japanese confectionery shops (*kashiya*). The fact that most of Japan's other major producers of kudzu powder buy their basic raw materials (in the form of partially refined kudzu powder) from Hiro Hachido places the company at a unique advantage in terms of competitive pricing; after paying harvesting and semi-processing commissions plus shipping costs, the other shops are forced to charge higher prices.

The manager of Hiro Hachido, Mr. Taguchi, is very friendly and hospitable, has a deep feeling for kudzu and other natural foods, and has had many years of experience in kudzu powder production. Though production is on a large scale and modern equipment is used, the company has maintained a fairly traditional orientation and still believes in slow, natural processing as described in chapter 4.

Inoue Sakae Shoten, Kuzu-cho 107, Gose-shi, Nara-ken 639-22. Tel: 07456-7-1666. Mr. Inoue, director.

Started in the 1870s, this company is now in its fourth generation. Using semiprocessed kudzu starch (40% moisture) from Kyushu, it produces 330,000 pounds of real kudzu powder each year, plus 550,000 pounds of a mixture containing 10 to 15 percent real kudzu powder and the remainder potato starch; these products are sold under the brand names "Tengoku" and "Kuzu-jiro." The company also sells pickles, glutinous yams, and other products from the nearby mountains and forests.

Morino Yoshino Kudzu Honpo, Ouda-machi, Ouda-gun, Nara-ken 633-21. Tel: 07458-3-0002. Mr. Tosuke Morino, director. The oldest and most experienced company making kudzu powder in Japan, this four-hundred-year-old-shop has been in the same family for twenty generations. Located in the small and rustic town of Ouda, the company employs about nine workers and produces about 82,500 pounds of real kudzu powder each year. The shop buys semi-processed kudzu starch and refines it into a natural product sold under the brand name "Miyuki." Morino takes pride in its long, well-documented history, the purity of its mountain stream water, and the many awards its kudzu powder has won. The company offers several free brochures on kudzu powder and its history, and the history of the shop. Many recipes and medicinal preparations are also included.

About two hundred years ago, the eleventh-generation master of the shop developed a life-long interest in medicinal herbs. On the steep hillside behind the shop he cultivated a very large and lovely garden, planting hundreds of varieties of herbal flowers which are still well labeled and cared for. In the shade of a grove of cedars at the top of the hill, he built a simple tea house and study which also still remain well maintained for visitors to enjoy. A later master of the shop is reported to have offered Yoshino Kudzu to a new emperor upon his ascension to the throne. The traditional shop and herb garden are shown on page 95.

At present, most of the kudzu powder at Morino is processed in open-top, rectangular concrete tanks set in an outdoor courtyard. Today the kudzu starch and water mixture is stirred by a mixing machine mounted overhead on railroad tracks which run along both sides of the large tanks. The hundreds of beautiful old wooden tubs which were used up until several years ago lay stacked nearby.

Kurokawa Honké, Ouda-machi, Ouda-gun, Nara-ken 633-21. Tel: 07458-3-0025. Mr. Jutaro Kurokawa, director. Located almost across the street from Morino, this ten-generations-old shop is known for having most successfully preserved the traditional tools and methodology for making kudzu powder and for producing a very high-quality product, the finest grade of which—sold under the brand name "Zuiki"—commands the highest price of any kudzu powder in Japan and has been given the great honor of being used by the imperial household. The shop, which employs eight workers, uses half-processed raw material from Kyushu and produces about 66,000 pounds of real kudzu powder each year.

Mr. Kurokawa, the president of the Kudzu Association for Nara and Mie Prefectures, speaks some English and is well informed and most helpful. The floor of his beautiful shop is covered with antique handmade wooden tubs (each about 2 feet deep and 3 feet in diameter) which are still used daily. Except

for the large propellers used to mix the kudzu starch and water in 5-foot-deep, 5-foot-diameter wooden vats, and a drying room with a fan and artificial heating to be used whenever it rains or snows, there is little evidence of modern machinery or technology at Kurokawa Honke.

Takagi Kyusuké Shoten, Akizuki-machi, Amagi-shi, Fukuoka-ken 838. Tel: 09462-5-0215. Mr. Takagi Kyusuké. Founded in 1819 and now in its eighth generation, this company is owned by a cousin of the owner of Hiro Hachido. Takagi Kyusuké produces about 40,000 pounds of real kudzu powder yearly, sold under the brand name "Hirokyu." They also produce "Kyusuké Kudzu," consisting of 100 percent sweet-potato starch (*kansho denpun*); production figures are not available.

The traditional herb garden and kudzu shop at Morino Yoshino Kudzu Honpo in the town of Ouda in Nara Prefecture. The lovely garden, planted over two hundred years ago, is still open to the public. The shop is one of the most famous in Japan.

MAKERS OF KUDZU NOODLES IN JAPAN

Kitamura Seimenjo, Kaya-hara 261, Oaza, Sakurai-shi, Nara-ken 633. Tel: 07444-2-6300 (or 9803). This company produces the "Itomaki Kuzukiri" brand.

Kuzuhidé, Kawara-machi 4-12, Takaoka-shi, Toyama-ken 933. Tel: 0766-22-1314. Mr. Hideo Takeuchi, owner. Distributed by Manto, Inc., Tokyo. Tel: 03-841-5914. Their product contains 30 percent real kudzu powder.

Miwa Somen Yamamoto, Inc., Hashi-naka 1046, Sakurai-shi, Nara-ken 639-01. Tel: 07444-2-6661. This company makes a variety of kudzu noodles containing 20 percent real kudzu powder and 80 percent sweet-potato starch; Kudzu Konnyaku containing 50 percent each real kudzu powder and konnyaku (the starch of a yam-like tuber); and Kudzu Konnyaku Noodles (*kudzu shirataki*) containing 10 percent kudzu powder and 90 percent konnyaku.

RESTAURANTS FEATURING KUDZU CUISINE

Sesame Tofu is served at many Zen temple restaurants, while Kudzu-zakura is available at most Japanese confectioneries during the early summer.

Goemon, Hongomagome 1-1-26, Bunkyo-ku, Tokyo. Tel: 03-811-2015. Sugamo Station. Delicious Sesame Tofu in a classically beautiful atmosphere.

Kagizen, Shijo-dori & Hanami-koji, Kitagawa 264, Gion-machi, Higashiyama-ku, Kyoto. Tel: 075-561-8743. Famous for its artistically served, homemade Kudzu Noodles in Chilled Molasses Sauce (see chapter 2).

Nishiyama Sodo, Tenryuji-nai, Arashiyama, Ukyo-ku, Kyoto. Tel: 075-861-1609. Located in the countryside west of Kyoto, this charming outdoor restaurant is renowned for its Zen Temple Cookery and Sesame Tofu.

KUDZU SCHOLARS IN JAPAN

Miyamoto Tsuneichi, Nihon Kanko Bunka Kenkyujo, Taito 1-12-11, Taito-ku, Tokyo 110. Tel: 03-832-0982. A noted scholar of Japanese folk crafts and customs; director of the above institute, which furthers such study.

Tsugawa Hyoe, Kobe Daigaku, Nogaku-bu, Sakumotsu-gaku Kenkyushitsu. 1 Rokko Daimachi, Nada-ku, Kobe-shi 657. Tel: 078-881-1212. A university professor in the faculty of agriculture, Dr. Tsugawa is probably the foremost authority on the history, utilization, and biology of kudzu in Japan.

PEOPLE CONNECTED WITH KUDZU CLOTH

Foster, Ann, Yurt Foundation, Bucks Harbor, ME 04618 U.S.A. Ann has studied kudzu fiber production and weaving for several years in Japan and has a color film on the subject.

Goto Shoichi, 3-22-11 Mikuni Honcho, Yodogawa-ku, Osaka, Japan. Tel: 06-952-8851. A master of dyeing kudzu cloth, 80-year-old Goto is also the author of one of Japan's most esteemed books on traditional textiles.

Kawade Moichi, Nito-machi 813, Kakkegawa-shi, Shizuoka-ken 436 Japan. Tel: 05372-4-2021. The fourth-generation owner of Japan's most famous shop producing kudzu cloth, Mr. Kawade has two excellent color films on the subject, plus numerous other resource materials.

Odani Tsugio, 2 Enkojiyama-cho, Monzen, Saga, Nison-in, Ukyo-ku, Kyoto-fu, Japan. Tel: 075-872-9174. This master weaver is famous for his kudzu kimonos.

COMPANIES EXPORTING KUDZU POWDER FROM JAPAN

Mitoku, C.P.O. Box 780, Tokyo 100-91. Tel: 03-201-6706. Mr. Akiyoshi Kazama, director.

Muso Shokuhin, 1-43 Otedori, Higashi-ku, Osaka 540. Tel: 06-945-0511. Mr. Teizo Okada, director. Both Mitoku and Muso currently buy all their kudzu powder from Hiro Hachido (above).

SOURCES OF AMERICAN KUDZU ROOT

The Fmali Co., 831 Alman Ave., Santa Cruz, CA 95060

COMPANIES IMPORTING KUDZU POWDER TO THE WEST

NORTH AMERICA

Chico-san Food Co., 1144 West First St., Chico CA 95926. Tel: 916-342-6770.

Erewhon Natural Foods, 33 Farnsworth St., Boston MA 02210. Tel: 617-542-1358.

Janus Natural Foods, 1523 Airport Way South, Seattle WA 98134. Tel: 206-624-1084.

The Well, 795 West Hedding St., San Jose CA 95126. Tel: 408-247-4800.

EUROPE

Lima Foods, Edgar Gevaertdreff 10, 9830 St. Martens-Latem, Belgium. Tel: (09) 82.41.76.

SOURCES OF KUDZU ROOT TEA

Chan Ping Herb Tea Store, 127-A Ma Tan We Rd., Kowloon, Hong Kong.

Chin Chow Herb Tea Shop, 73-D Kings Rd., Hong Kong.

Herbal Tea Co., 440 Judah St., San Francisco CA 94122. Tel: 415-564-8651.

Kinokuniya Kanyakkyoku, 1-2-4 Soto Kanda, Chiyoda-ku, Tokyo 110, Japan. Tel: 03-255-2771.

SOURCES OF KUDZU VINES & SEEDS

George W. Park Seed Co., P.O. Box 31, Greenwood, SC 29647. A supplier of kudzu seeds; 50 for about 75 cents.

Savage Farm Nursery, P.O. Box 125-OFA, McMinnville TN 37110. A supplier of kudzu vines; about 29 cents each plus postage.

Bibliography

WORKS IN ENGLISH ABOUT KUDZU

A Barefoot Doctor's Manual. Washington, D.C.: U.S. Department of Health, Education, and Welfare, 1974. Originally published by the Institute of Traditional Chinese Medicine of Honan Province. Information about medicinal kudzu root.

Ahlgren, G. H. *Forage Crops.* 2nd ed. New York: McGraw-Hill, 1956. One of the best sources of agricultural information about the kudzu plant; contains an extensive bibliography.

Alexander, E. D., and Preston, J. B. *Kudzu.* Georgia Agricultural Extension Service, Circular No. 331 (1950).

Bailey, R. Y. *Kudzu for Erosion Control in the Southeast.* U.S. Department of Agriculture, Farmers Bulletin No. 1840 (1939; 2nd ed. rev., 1958). A thirty-page manual containing numerous photographs and describing in detail the planting and use of kudzu for erosion control, green manure, and fodder. Out of print.

———. "The Use of Kudzu on Critical Slopes." *Soil Conservation* 5(39):49.

Bennet, H. H. *Soil Conservation.* New York: McGraw-Hill, 1939. The major work of one of kudzu's great popularizers.

Bennet, H. W., and Crockett, S. P. "Kudzu Used as Temporary Pasturage." *Mississippi Farm Research* 7(47):1–2.

Blackwell, J. "The Vine That Ate the South." *Georgia,* November 1973. Humorous.

Brender, E. V. "Controls of Honeysuckle and Kudzu." USDA Forest Service Station Paper 120. Southeastern Forest Experimental Station, Ashville (1961), pp. 1–8.

Brooklyn Botanic Gardens. "Kudzu." *Brooklyn Botanic Record,* Winter 1974–75.

Burt, A. "How Kudzu Conquered the South." *Miami Herald,* 1976.

Cargould, P. R. "Kudzu in the North." *The Land* 4(45):456–58.

Ching-chang Chuang, Chia Huang. *The Leguminosae of Taiwan: For Pasture and Soil Improvement.* 87. National Taiwan University (1965).

Clemson College. "Kudzu in South Carolina: Its Value for Forage, Grazing, and Soil Improvement." Clemson College Extension Service Circular 164 (1938).

Cope, Channing. *Front Porch Farmer.* Atlanta: Turner E. Smith, 1949. The runaway bestseller that made kudzu famous.

———. "Kudzu." *Farm Quarterly.* (5(50):56.

Crops and Soils. "Kill Kudzu . . ." March 1955.

———. "Kudzu Produces Good Pasture on Dry Lands Even in Dry Periods." January 1952.

———. "Kudzu Up North." December 1952.

———. "Kudzu Weak . . ." March 1953.

Dacey, G. H. "Be Cautious with Kudzu." *Country Life* 31(17):100–102.

Davis, D. E., and Funderbunk, H. H. "Eradication of Kudzu." *Weeds* 12(64):62–63.

Davis, R. L., and Young, W. C. "Kudzu 23: A New Fine-textured Variety." *Soil Conservation* 14(51):279–80.

Encyclopedia of Organic Gardening. Emmaus PA: Rodale Press, 1971. Contains an analysis of cured kudzu hay.

Funchess, M. J., and Tisdale, H. B. "Kudzu for Hay." Auburn Agricultural Experiment Station, 35th Annual Report (1924), pp. 5–6.

Hendrickson, Bert M. "Kudzu Legume Vine is Lush Forage on Eroded Wasteland of the South." *What's New in Crops and Soils,* December 1949, p. 26.

Howard, F. *Landscaping with Vines.* New York: Macmillan, 1959.

Kipps, M. S. *Production of Field Crops.* 6th ed. New York: McGraw-Hill, 1970. Contains a brief discussion of kudzu with several references.

"Kudzu." *USDA Yearbook,* Washington, D.C.: 1948, pp. 703–726.

Lancaster, Robert R. *Annual Lespedezas.* Texas Agricultural Extension Circular No. 178 (1949).

Lord, Russel. "Kudzu: Another Agricultural Miracle." *Country Book Magazine,* Autumn 1944. Reprinted (condensed) in *Readers Digest,* January 1945. A highly readable description of the ways kudzu is used in the United States for erosion control, green manure, and fodder.

———. "Kudzu Marches On." *The Land* 3(44):369.

Lowrey, J. C. *Kudzu.* Auburn University Extension Service Circular No. 161. Auburn, Alabama (1921).

McKee, R., and Stephens J. L. *Kudzu as a Farm Crop.* USDA Farmers Bulletin No. 1923 (1948).

Moulton, R. H. "Kudzu, the Latest Forage Plant." *Scientific American,* supplement, vol. 88 (1919), p. 365.

Nixon, W. M. "Plant Kudzu from Seed." *What's New in Crops and Soils* 1(48):14–15.

O'Brien, R. E., and Skelton, D. W. *The Production and Utilization of Kudzu.* Mississippi State Agricultural Experiment Station Bulletin No. 483 (1946).

Ohwi, J. *Flora of Japan.* Washington, D.C.: Smithsonian Institution, 1965.

"Oriental Immigrant from the Plant Kingdom." *Illustrated World* 34(20):279.

Piper, C. V. *Kudzu.* USDA Circular No. 89 (1920).

Porterfield, W. M. "The Principal Chinese Vegetable Foods and Food Plants of Chinatown Markets." *Economic Botany,* Vol. 5 (1951).

Preters, A. J., et al. *Sericea and Other Perennial Lespedezas for Forage and Soil Conservation.* USDA Circular No. 863 (1950).

Purseglove, J. W. *Tropical Crops: Dicotyledons.* Vol. 1. New York: John Wiley & Sons, 1968. Contains a discussion of the plants to which Japanese kudzu is related.

"Reader Responses to Kudzu." *Organic Gardening and Farming.* March, June, and September 1976.

Richardson, E. C. "The Effects of Fertilizer on Stand and Yield of Kudzu on Depleted Soils." *Journal of the American Society of Agronomy* 37(45):763–70.

―――. "The Use of Kudzu in a Rotation System." *Soil Conservation*, Vol. 8 (1943).

Rowalt, E. M. "Kudzu Is This Farmer's Friend." *Soil Conservation*, Vol. 1 (1936).

Stevens, R. W. "Kudzu: The Versatile Wonder-Bean." *Organic Farmer*, Vol. 4 (1953).

Sturkie, D. G., and Grimes, J. C. *Kudzu: Its Value and Use in Alabama*. Alabama Agricultural Experiment Station Circular No. 83 (1939).

Tabor, P. V. "Observations of Kudzu Seedlings" and "Seed Production by Kudzu in the Southeastern United States during 1941." *Journal of the American Society of Agronomy*, Vol. 34 (1942).

―――, and Susott, A. W. "Zero to Thirty Million Mile-a-Minute Seedlings." *Soil Conservation*, Vol. 7 (1941).

Williams, C. G. *Kudzu, a Failure in Ohio*. Ohio Agricultural Experiment Station Bulletin No. 382 (1924).

Winberry, J. J., and Jones, D. M. "Rise and Decline of the 'Miracle Vine' Kudzu in the Southern Landscape." *Southern Geographer*, Vol. 13, No. 2 (November 1973). Perhaps the best general survey to date of the history of kudzu in America.

Woodhead, Henry. "Happy Birthday Miracle Vine." *Atlanta Journal and Constitution*, September 19, 1976. An extremely humorous and informative review of kudzu's bizarre first century in America.

WORKS IN ENGLISH CONTAINING RECIPES

Aihara, Cornellia. *The Chico-san Cookbook*. Chico CA: Chico-san Inc., 1972. Contains over twenty Japanese-style recipes using kudzu powder.

Keys, John. *Chinese Herbs: Their Botany, Chemistry, and Pharmacodynamics*. Tokyo: Charles E. Tuttle. 1976. Probably the most reliable and comprehensive book on Chinese herbal medicine currently available in English.

Li Shih-Chen. *Chinese Medicinal Herbs*. San Francisco: Georgetown Press, 1973.

Muramoto, Noboru. *Healing Ourselves*. New York City: Avon, 1973. Contains good information about medicinal kudzu root teas and kudzu creams.

Ohsawa, Georges. *Zen Cookery*. Los Angeles: Ignoramus Press, 1966. Contains a number of interesting medicinal kudzu recipes.

―――. *Zen Macrobiotics; The Philosophy of Oriental Medicine*. Vol I. Los Angeles: Ohsawa Foundation, 1965. Contains a great deal of information about the medicinal uses of kudzu powder.

Ohsawa, Lima. *The Art of Just Cooking*. Brookline: Autumn Press, 1974. Contains a number of interesting recipes using kudzu powder.

Shurtleff, W.R. *The Book of Tofu*. Brookline: Autumn Press, 1975.

―――. *The Book of Miso*. Brookline: Autumn Press, 1976. Both books have many kudzu recipes.

Toguchi, Masaru. *Oriental Herbal Wisdom*, New York: Pyramid, 1973. Contains recipes for medicinal kudzu root teas.

WORKS IN JAPANESE

We used the following Japanese works extensively in our research. For easy reference, we list them here in order of the English translation of their titles.

Encyclopedia of Ancient Medicinal Plants (*Kojiruien; Shokubutsu Bu-ichi*). 51 volumes. Tokyo: Yoshikawa Kobunkan, 1896. Contains detailed information about kudzu's medicinal uses in ancient times. It took the staff of the Ise Shrine thirty-five years to write this treasure trove of herbal lore, commissioned by the Japanese Ministry of Education.

Encyclopedia of Food and Drink (*Inshoku Jiten*). Tokyo: Heibonsha, 1972. Contains detailed information on the history and use of kudzu powder in Japanese cuisine.

History of Kudzu Utilization in Japan (*Kudzu no Shiyoshi: Kudzu-ko ni Tsuite*) by Tsugawa Hyoe. *Bulletin of Grassland Ecology Research Group*, no. 13 (1972). The best historical overview to date.

Kudzu Cloth (*Kudzu-fu*). A series of twelve articles about kudzu cloth in issues no. 1098 to 1109 (1975) of Kakegawa's local newspaper.

"Kudzu Cloth from Kakegawa" ("*Kakegawa no Kudzu-fu*") by Tonomura Kichinosuke. In *Kogei* [Industrial arts]. Tokyo: Nihon Mingei Kyokai, 1934.

Kudzu Fiber Filament Production (*Kudzu-o Seizo no Tebiki*). 1954. This 27-page booklet, written and published by an unknown Shinto priest, gives a detailed description of the basic process.

Kudzu: The Plant to Save Japan (*Kudzu: Nihon o Suku Shokubutsu*) by Mukaeda Toshio. Agricultural Resource Development Publishing Department, 264 Shimo Daita-machi, Setagaya-ku, Tokyo: 1953. A 64-page discussion of kudzu's value as a source of fertilizer and fodder. Out of print.

Macrobiotic Cookery (*Makurobiotiku Ryori*) by Ohsawa, Lima. Tokyo: Nihon C.I., 1971. Contains many simple but tasty recipes and medicinal preparations, using kudzu powder.

"Research concerning Kudzu Powder" ("*Kudzu-ko ni Kansuru Kenkyu*") by Shinoda Shoichi. In (*Nogyo Oyobi Engei*) [Farming and horticulture]. 35 volumes. Tokyo: Yokendo, 1960.

Traditional Japanese Textiles (*Nihon Dento Orimono Shusei*) by Goto Shoichi. Kyoto: Senshoku to Seikatsu-sha, 1974. This unique $500 book, accompanied by actual samples of each of the textiles it describes, contains numerous photographs and basic information about the production and history of the kudzu cloth made in both Kakegawa and Karatsu. Mr. Moichi Kawadé (see appendix b) has one copy.

"Yoshino Kudzu" in *Seishoku*, no. 6 (1976). Contains two detailed and well-illustrated articles: one describes the preparation of kudzu powder on a commercial scale; the other gives the results of laboratory tests proving that much of the kudzu powder sold in Japan is not real kudzu but rather potato starch.

World Encyclopedia (*Sekai Hyakka Jiten*). Tokyo: Heibonsha, 1975. Contains an extensive treatment of the history and many uses of kudzu powder and root.

Zen Temple Cookery (*Shojin Ryori*). Tokyo: Fujokai Shuppansha, 1972. Written by the head temple cooks of four of Japan's best-known Buddhist monasteries: Eiheiji, Sojiji, Daitokuji, and Tansenji. Contains a large number of simple yet imaginative recipes using kudzu powder.

FILMS ABOUT KUDZU

Kudzu: An offbeat, witty, informative documentary short about the vine which is devouring the South (16 minutes long, in 16mm, color). It features President Jimmy Carter, author James Dickey (*Deliverance*), and a diverse cast of characters. It won the Special Jury Award Gold Medal for Documentary Shorts at the 1976 Virgin Islands International Film Festival, St. Thomas, V.I., and was nominated for the Academy Award. Produced, directed, and edited by Marjie Short; funded by a grant from the National Endowment for the Arts. Available for rental. Contact: Marjie Short, Short Productions, 13 Glenwood Ave. #3, Cambridge, MA. 02139, Tel: 617-661-2509.

Kudzu Cloth: A two-part silent documentary (each part 25 minutes long, in 8mm, color) filmed in the Japanese village of Kakegawa by Mr. Moichi Kawadé, head of the local weaver's cooperative. Part I on extraction of kudzu fiber is available for rental in the United States from Ann Foster (see appendix B). Part II on weaving of the different cloths is available for rental only in Japan from Mr. Kawade (see appendix B).

Japanese crest, stylized kudzu flower

Glossary

The following Japanese-style ingredients and cooking utensils, referred to throughout this book, are widely available in the West at Japanese food markets and a growing number of natural and health food stores.

Agar: A sea vegetable gelatin made from the genera *Gelidium* and *Gracilaria*. Sold in the form of flakes, bars, powder, or strands.

Ankaké: A thickened sauce seasoned with natural soy sauce (shoyu); usually contains some sweetening.

Azuki: A small red bean used in confections or steamed with rice (the term *aduki* is a misspelling).

Bancha: Green tea made from the leaves and twigs of three-year-old tea bushes.

Beefsteak leaf *(shiso)*: An herblike aromatic leaf available in red and green species; the red are used in the preparation of salt plums.

Daikon: Giant Japanese white radish.

Dashi: Soup stock generally made from kombu and in many cases bonita flakes or tiny fish.

Gomashio: Sesame salt.

Kabocha: Also called Hokkaido pumpkin, this deliciously sweet winter squash with its white yellow-to-orange meat actually originated in Maine; it was introduced to Japan in the early 1800s.

Kabu: Small (3-inch-diameter), heart-shaped, pure-white turnips having a mild, slightly sweet flavor.

Kakkon: Dried diced cubes of kudzu root.

Kanten: *see* Agar.

Katakuriko: A popular traditional cooking starch made from the roots of the dog-tooth violet. Modern products so labeled generally contain only potato starch.

Kinako: Full-fat roasted soy flour.

Koko: Grain coffee.

Kombu: A Japanese sea vegetable of the genus *Laminaria* somewhat resembling kelp; used mostly in the preparation of soup stocks and in stews.

Matcha: *see* Powdered green tea.

Mirin: Sweet sake used only for cooking. For each tablespoon of mirin called for, you may substitute ½ teaspoon honey and 2 teaspoons sake or pale dry sherry. Or you may substitute 1½ teaspoons honey and 2½ teaspoons water.

Miso: Fermented soybean paste. The three basic Japanese varieties are red, barley, and Hatcho miso. For detailed information, see *The Book of Miso*.

Mochi: Cakes of pounded, steamed glutinous rice. Kudzu confections are often made to have a similar appearance and texture.

Mu tea: A mixture of fragrant herbs used also for its medicinal properties. The basic variety contains peony root, Japanese parsley root, hoelen, cinnamon, licorice, peach kernels, gingerroot, Japanese ginseng, and rhenannia. A more elaborate variety contains in addition mikan peel, cnicus, atractylis, cypress, cloves, moutan, and coptis.

Nori: Paper-thin, purplish-black sheets made from the sea vegetable laver (*Porphyra*).

Powdered green tea *(matcha)*: Finest-quality green tea ground to a powder between stone wheels. Used in the traditional tea ceremony.

Salt plum *(umeboshi)*: A partially ripe plum, salt-pickled with red beefsteak leaves and used as both a tart seasoning and a highly alkaline natural medicine.

Shiso: *see* Beefsteak leaves.

Shoyu: All-purpose Japanese-style fermented soy sauce, made from soybeans, wheat, salt, and water. Not to be confused with the low-quality, domestic, synthetic soy sauce made without fermentation from hydrolyzed vegetable protein, caramel coloring, corn syrup, salt, and water. This latter type, generally sold under Chinese brand names, constitutes two-thirds of all soy sauce sold in America. Natural shoyu, imported to America and often sold as "tamari" (although real tamari is actually a completely different product), is made from whole soybeans aged in cedar vats at the natural temperature of the environment for at least one year; no preservatives are added. "Regular" shoyu, also a high-quality product (produced mostly by Kikkoman in America), costs about two-thirds as much as natural shoyu; defatted soybean meal is substituted for whole soybeans and the product is aged in epoxy-lined steel tanks in a slightly heated (75°) room for six months. The domestic commercial variety contains perservatives, but the imported low-salt variety is preservative-free.

Soba: Japanese-style buckwheat noodles.

Soy sauce: *see* Shoyu.

Suribachi: An earthenware mortar with unglazed, serrated grooves. Used with a wooden pestle.

Tahini: A smooth, creamy paste made from unroasted (or very lightly roasted), hulled white sesame seeds. Due to the removal of the calcium-rich hulls, tahini is not as nutritious as sesame butter, and some commercial processes use caustic soda in the cleaning and hulling process. Contains 19 percent protein.

Tekka miso: A crumbly, savory seasoning prepared by sautéeing diced vegetables (burdock root, carrot, lotus root, gingerroot, etc.) in sesame oil together with Hatcho miso. Easily made at home (see *The Book of Miso*) and also available commercially.

Tofu: Soybean curd. Regular tofu comes in 12-to-16-ounce cakes, having a consistency like that of a soft cheese or very firm yogurt. Other varieties available in the West include: silken tofu, deep-fried tofu cutlets, burgers, and pouches, grilled tofu, wine-fermented tofu, Chinese-style firm tofu, and dried-frozen tofu. For detailed information see *The Book of Tofu*.

Umeboshi: *see* Salt plum.

Wasabi: Green Japanese horseradish, sold as a powder which is mixed with water just before use, or as a 4-inch-long root which is grated and served fresh.

Washi: Japanese paper made by a chemical-free natural process from the fibers from the bark of either the *kozo* (paper mulberry) or *mitsumata* (*Edgewortha crythantha*) trees. Soft, strong, and pure, it is widely used for steaming and serving foods.

Yannoh: A grain coffee.

Index

ABOUT THE AUTHORS

William Shurtleff and Akiko Aoyagi spent their formative years on opposite sides of the Pacific. Born in California in 1941, Bill was educated at Stanford, is a veteran of the Peace Corps (Biafra), and spent 2½ years at the Tassajara Zen Mountain Center under former head abbot Shunryu Suzuki Roshi. Akiko was born in Tokyo in 1950, received her education at the Quaker-run Friend's School and the Women's College of Arts, and has worked as an illustrator in Japan's modern fashion industry.

Since 1971 they have worked together to introduce to the West traditional East Asian foods which they feel can play a key role in helping to solve the world food crisis, while providing high-quality low-cost nutrition for people everywhere. Their writings are uniquely holistic and in tune with a growing interest in traditional food craftsmanship, the integration of one's occupation with personal/spiritual growth, and the evolution of a simpler, more satisfying lifestyle. Rooted in their common practice of meditation and simultaneous commitment to social action, their work attempts to complete the circle linking East and West. It connects us with the most creative aspects of our ancient past and aims to tie all people together as brothers and sisters. Their nationwide tours, which feature cooking classes and lectures on soybean foods and sea vegetables have drawn very favorable response, and their work as consultants for the establishment of American tofu and miso shops is quickly showing concrete results. Their previous writings include *The Book of Tofu* and *The Book of Miso*. They were married in March, 1977.

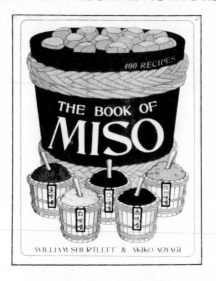